Waters Less Traveled

Florida History and Culture

Florida A&M University, Tallahassee
Florida Atlantic University, Boca Raton
Florida Gulf Coast University, Ft. Myers
Florida International University, Miami
Florida State University, Tallahassee
University of Central Florida, Orlando
University of Florida, Gainesville
University of North Florida, Jacksonville
University of South Florida, Tampa
University of West Florida, Pensacola

The Florida History and Culture Series
Edited by Raymond Arsenault and Gary R. Mormino

The Stranahans of Ft. Lauderdale: A Pioneer Family of New River, by Harry A. Kersey Jr. (2003)

Death in the Everglades: The Murder of Guy Bradley, America's First Martyr to Environmentalism, by Stuart B. McIver (2003)

Jacksonville: The Consolidation Story, from Civil Rights to the Jaguars, by James B. Crooks (2004)

The Seminole Wars: The Nation's Longest Indian Conflict, by John and Mary Lou Missall (2004)

The Mosquito Wars: A History of Mosquito Control in Florida, by Gordon Patterson (2004)

The Seasons of Real Florida, by Jeff Klinkenberg (2004, first paperback edition 2005)

Land of Sunshine, State of Dreams: A Social History of Modern Florida, by Gary Mormino (2005)

Paradise Lost? The Environmental History of Florida, edited by Jack E. Davis and Raymond Arsenault (2005)

Frolicking Bears, Wet Vultures, and Other Oddities: A New York City Journalist in Nineteenth-Century Florida, edited by Jerald T. Milanich (2005)

Waters Less Traveled: Exploring Florida's Big Bend Coast, by Doug Alderson (2005)

University Press of Florida
Gainesville · Tallahassee · Tampa · Boca Raton
Pensacola · Orlando · Miami · Jacksonville · Ft. Myers

WATERS LESS TRAVELED

Exploring Florida's Big Bend Coast

Doug Alderson

Foreword by Gary R. Mormino and Raymond Arsenault

Copyright 2005 by Doug Alderson
Printed in the United States of America on recycled, acid-free paper

10 09 08 07 06   05 6 5 4 3 2 1

A record of cataloging-in-publication data is available from the
Library of Congress.

ISBN 0-8130-2903-1

The University Press of Florida is the scholarly publishing agency
for the State University System of Florida, comprising Florida A&M
University, Florida Atlantic University, Florida Gulf Coast University,
Florida International University, Florida State University, University
of Central Florida, University of Florida, University of North Florida,
University of South Florida, and University of West Florida.

University Press of Florida
15 Northwest 15th Street
Gainesville, FL 32611-2079
http://www.upf.com

To John and Jeanne Alderson, my parents. You were there for me.

CONTENTS

FOREWORD

Waters Less Traveled: Exploring Florida's Big Bend Coast is the latest volume in a series devoted to the study of Florida history and culture. During the past half century, the burgeoning growth and increased national and international visibility of Florida have sparked a great deal of popular interest in the state's past, present, and future. As the favorite destination of hordes of tourists and as the new home for millions of retirees, immigrants, and transplants, modern Florida has become a demographic, political, and cultural bellwether.

A state of vast distances and distant strangers, Florida needs more citizens who care about the welfare of this special place and its people. We hope this series helps newcomers and old-timers appreciate and understand Florida. The University Press of Florida established the Florida History and Culture Series in an effort to provide an accessible and attractive format for the publication of works related to the Sunshine State.

As coeditors of the series, we are deeply committed to the creation of an eclectic but carefully crafted set of books that will provide the field of Florida studies with a fresh focus and encourage Florida researchers and writers to consider the broader implications and context of their work. The series includes monographs, memoirs, anthologies, and travelogues. And, while the series features books of historical interest, we encourage authors researching Florida's environment, politics, and popular or material culture to submit their manuscripts as well. We want each book to retain a distinct personality and voice, but at the same time we hope to foster a sense of community and collaboration among Florida scholars.

Doug Alderson has accomplished something that every writer hopes to achieve. In *Waters Less Traveled*, he takes readers to places that most of us have never visited and can only imagine: Spring Warrior Creek, Bonita Beach, Rock Island, and Sponge Point. By sea kayak and footpaths, he explores Florida's Big Bend, a region of rugged beauty and extraordinary diversity. From the oyster banks of the Apalachicola Bay to the ghost towns and old saltworks of Cedar Key, Alderson provides commentary on Big Bend folkways and history.

Florida's Big Bend provides stirring tales of survival and persistence, as well as heartbreaking chapters of betrayal and disillusionment. After centuries of boom and bust, stagnation and isolation, St. George Island, Carrabelle, and Steinhatchee have been discovered. The St. Joe Company looms ominously over the area. Alderson deftly balances the social and economic conflict that has accompanied growth and prosperity. In places like Apalachicola, Horseshoe Beach, and Cedar Key, new money and waterfront condominiums often clash with family fish camps and tradition. The Fenholloway, once one of the state's prettiest streams and home to resorts touting the water's mineral properties, has become polluted by industrial effluent. In Dixie County, where abandoned turpentine camps stand vigil over a haunted past, drug smugglers and Land Rovers more recently roamed the piney woods and marshes.

Waters Less Traveled: Exploring Florida's Big Bend Coast documents a joyous water journey, bringing to life a cast of colorful characters and unforgettable places. Alderson joins Al Burt, Jeff Klinkenberg, and Bill Belleville, a distinguished group of Florida authors who have mastered the art of writing about place.

Raymond Arsenault and Gary R. Mormino, Series Editors

PREFACE AND ACKNOWLEDGMENTS

In researching this book, it quickly became apparent that grasping the history, natural attributes, and cultures of Florida's Big Bend Coast was no easy task. I sifted through libraries, museums, historical societies, and private collections. I talked with scientists, old-timers, fishermen, and tale-tellers. Each source helped to resolve mysteries, and some raised more questions. While this book is the first comprehensive look at Florida's wildest stretch of coastline, it is by no means an exhaustive study. There is more to uncover and explore.

My most challenging task was writing about the Fenholloway River and its ongoing pollution from a pulp mill. It proved far more difficult than paddling for nine days in a sea kayak. Trying to balance my own environmental sensitivities with a concern for the economic welfare and long-term health of the folks in Taylor County was daunting. I hope the end result is fair and accurate. Any perceived slant is strictly my own and not the position of any particular organization, business, or government agency.

I owe many people a great deal of gratitude for this book. First, a big hug to my ever-supportive wife, Cyndi, and my daughter, Cheyenne. Working toward being a writer can be both a blessing and a curse; it helps to have the backing of one's family.

A big thanks to Liz Sparks, my kayaking companion along the Big Bend coast. Without her help, this book would not have been possible in its current form. Her humor and insightfulness added a great deal to the trip, and the book.

I appreciate Susan Cerulean for her strong encouragement early on and for providing invaluable editorial feedback. Jerrie Lindsey, my supervisor at the Florida Fish and Wildlife Conservation Commission (FWC), was supportive as well. A portion of the royalties from this book is being donated to the Wildlife Foundation of Florida, Inc., in order to support nature-based recreation opportunities on lands managed by the FWC.

I wish to thank Julie Brashears, Jeff Chanton, Julie Hauserman, Bob and Jamie Hayes, Skip Livingston, Ken Mick, Lucy Morgan, Dan Penton, Anne and Jack Rudloe, and Mike Wisenbaker for their input and support. I also appreciate Meredith Morris-Babb and the other good folks at the University Press of Florida.

Throughout the writing of this book, residents of the Big Bend Coast have earned my respect and gratitude. Many have been extremely helpful in uncovering information and allowing me into their homes to glimpse their lives and family history. Researching this book has been like a literary treasure hunt, with each person I've interviewed giving me greater understanding and providing clues as to my next step. A few of those helpful coastal residents include Preston Chavous, Evonne Cline, Henry Garcia, Shug Magnum, James Pittman, and Billy Sullivan.

My only regret is that this book had to end. It's been a rewarding journey.

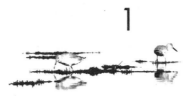

FIRST OYSTER

My initiation to the beauty and stark realities of north Florida's Gulf Coast revolved around a culinary challenge—the raw oyster.

Soon after moving to Florida from Illinois at age eleven, I joined the Boy Scouts. As my first full Florida summer approached, a plan emerged to do a "survival campout" on a remote island known as St. George, just south of East Point and at the western fringe of Florida's Big Bend.

Ken, as he liked to be called by young and old alike, was a unique scout-master. He often challenged us in exciting ways, mixing his background as a tough and disciplined U.S. Marine with a boyhood sense of adventure. We had already camped for two days in a wild cave near Marianna, a trip that included a long exploration of the cave's interior and a challenging return trip with lights turned off. A survival campout would build upon that experience.

"What will we eat?" someone asked as we discussed the idea at our July troop meeting.

"That's the whole idea. You have to find your own food and water," said Ken. "I know of an artesian well on the island, and there's plenty of oysters in Apalachicola Bay."

Hmm, oysters, I thought. I had never eaten an oyster, but the idea of surviving off the land—or from the water—appealed to me. "The Indians used to travel for days on a little bit of jerky and parched corn," said Ken.

A bright-faced Native American boy named David perked up. "My ancestors sure didn't eat much," he said, laughing nervously. David was the first full-blooded Native American I had met and one of the few to live in north Florida since the Indian removal period of the early to mid-1800s. I was eager to try anything Native Americans had done.

Ken added a stipulation to the campout: "All the supplies you need must fit into a half-gallon milk carton," he said. Recommended items included a pocketknife, fish line and hooks, matches, compass, toilet paper, and hard candy to help alleviate thirst and hunger pains. After the troop meeting, a boy told me privately that he planned to squish a stack of sandwiches into his carton, something I considered absurd until we were well into the campout.

The date of the campout was a weekend in mid-August, just before school was to begin. It didn't dawn on me during the planning session that we were undertaking our survival trip to a sun-drenched barrier island during the hottest month of the year. Temperatures could easily exceed a hundred degrees; humidity levels would be on par with the temperature. Mercifully, we would be allowed to pitch tents to keep out insects.

On the morning of the campout, we drove to the eastern end of St. George Island and set up camp. This wild half of the island would eventually be developed into a premier Florida state park, but at the time there were no bathrooms, showers, water faucets, picnic tables, or other amenities. We eager-faced Scouts were the only campers in this stark landscape of weathered slash pines, endless rows of sand dunes, and blue water.

After pitching tents, Ken announced that obtaining drinking water had to be our first priority. Our communal jug contained only enough life-sustaining liquid for a few sips per person.

With empty canteens, we began a long hike down a blinding sugar-sand road toward the artesian well. We often ducked into sparse shade provided by pines and shrubs; the sun had become hot and unforgiving. Those who were barefoot scurried faster to the shady spots. Our skin began turning a beet-red.

Within a mile, my throat was parched and my stomach growling. In my short life, I had missed meals only when I was dreadfully sick; water had always been available. The idea of a wild artesian well, whatever it was, was growing in its appeal. I envisioned it as a cool, clear gushing outflow of water, nothing short of the Fountain of Youth. The sweet liquid would wash down succulent oysters that resembled oval chunks of baked chicken in both taste and appearance. Breezes would kick up and blow away biting flies and sand gnats. We would feed on nature's bounty rather than nature's critters feeding on us.

I later learned that Native Americans generally moved inland from coastal areas during summer to escape insect swarms and blazing sun. So much for emulating those first island survivalists.

As hollow-sounding canteens banged against dusty legs, we struggled onward in what was fast becoming the Boy Scout version of the Bataan death march.

I daydreamed of visiting the island under different circumstances—on a beach trip with parents, brothers, and friends. Lounging on towels and blankets under a huge umbrella, we'd sip soda from plastic cups filled to the brim with ice, munch on fried chicken, and scoop out baked beans, mashed potatoes, and cole slaw from seemingly bottomless containers. Heaps of apple cobbler would follow . . .

We smelled the artesian well before we came upon it. Rotten eggs coupled with dissipating smoke from spent fireworks best described the smell. Putrid green algae covered our "Fountain of Youth." Scenes from western shows and movies flashed in my mind, ones that depicted half-dead desert wanderers reaching a watering hole only to find it poisoned, the ground littered with dead animals. One crazed sap, however, would ignore the warnings and dive facedown into the bad water, slurping ravenously. Soon we'd see him doubled over, retching, his face contorting grotesquely. Then he would die.

This scene did not play itself out with our group, fortunately. Ken refused to let us drink from the natural sulfur well, not that anyone volunteered.

We dragged ourselves to Apalachicola Bay, which was on the leeward side of the island. The bay continues to be one of the richest estuaries in North America, fed by the nutrient-rich Apalachicola River and protected by several barrier islands, including St. George. Oysters thrive in the special mixture of fresh- and salt water. It was a bounty Native Americans realized thousands of years before. They left behind long middens of shells, bones, and other refuse, prehistoric trash heaps where calcium-loving cedar trees now grow. Those early oysters were often eight to ten inches in length, more than double the size of modern-day oysters. That's because oyster tongers from the towns of Apalachicola and Eastpoint have steadily harvested the shellfish for more than a century and a half. Their ways have changed little.

Harvesters spend long days standing in a boat and pulling up oysters by hand with long-handled tongs. Helpers cull out undersized oysters and return them to the bay. The oyster tongers and commercial fishermen are a primary reason Apalachicola Bay has been carefully guarded from pollution and overdevelopment through the years. Human livelihoods depend on it.

"How are we gonna eat the oysters?" I asked Ken naively.

"Raw," he replied.

Raw meat? That didn't sound appetizing. "What do oysters taste like?"

He looked at me quizzically. "You've never had an oyster before?" His tone suggested that this was a hell of a time to try.

"Nope."

"You'll find out soon enough. Just don't chew when you put it in your mouth. Let it slide down your throat and then swallow."

"Yeah, it's just like a big booger!" a nearby boy crudely exclaimed. Ken gave him a stern look, but it was too late. My innocence was stirring up something in the other boys. They weren't quite like predatory hyenas sensing a kill—more like perched crows with a ringside seat.

We waded into the water, but a protruding shark fin prompted a quick retreat. "Probably just a sand or nurse shark," said Ken. "They won't hurt you." Still, I hung back. While living in Illinois, I had read a huge book that chronicled every reported shark attack off Florida's coast. I felt sure that a big shark would drag me underwater at the first opportunity, providing a new case study for the revised edition.

Ken and some other boys bravely waded a short distance and soon found an underwater oyster bar. They eagerly pried loose dark clusters of oysters, driven by hunger and a foreknowledge of their edibility. With a stout knife, Ken cracked open a big oyster and loosened the meat. I watched with keen interest and concealed horror as Ken's son Terry leaned his head back and let the slippery oval meat slide into his mouth. Then he swallowed. He glanced around to show that the feat had been accomplished without squeamishness.

"Hey, Doug, why don't you eat the next one?" challenged a boy. "You ain't chicken, are you?" Others offered similar encouragement.

"Okay," I said nervously. Perhaps I sensed an initiation of sorts. Upon passage, I could penetrate the inner sanctum of the troop, no longer relegated to the fringe with other new boys. Then I could more freely partake in crude language, bathroom humor, and mean-spirited pranks. It was behavior that tests the limits of adult tolerance—a multiyear outbreak of male adolescence.

Ken opened a palm-sized oyster and handed it to me. The wet meat jiggled in its perfect natural container. Somewhere inside this humble creation, I knew there was a beating heart.

"Now remember, don't chew until you get used to them," Ken reminded.

I looked at the oyster, glanced at the many eyes upon me, looked back at the oyster, then brought it to my lips. I tilted my head back. The slimy meat slid into my mouth and throat. It was worse than a booger! Far worse. I gagged. That brought the oyster back into my mouth. Panicky, I chewed. The oyster squished between my teeth. I thought of those oyster organs— the still-beating heart, the stomach, liver, and intestines . . . With those scrutinizing eyes upon me, however, I refused to spit it out. Not then. With strength I didn't know I possessed, I willed myself to swallow my first oyster.

I could not breathe.

"Want another one?" Ken asked. I shook my head in the negative. I turned and walked a ways on land, out of sight, and relieved myself of the recent contents of my stomach.

At least we wouldn't depend upon raw oysters, I thought.

My colleague Liz Sparks was showing me her checklist for our planned nine-day sea kayak trip along the Big Bend coast. We would begin at the Aucilla River and finish at the mouth of the Suwannee, covering more than a hundred miles. From Liz's list, I determined we would have an ample supply of freeze-dried and dried foods and several gallons of water per day, but I had other worries—storms, high winds, bugs, blazing sun. In case of an accident, most of the route was out of cell phone coverage, and coastal towns were two or three days apart. "I brought a flare gun," Liz assured me. "And I borrowed a marine radio. I just have to figure out how to use it."

Nine days? That was seven days longer than my Boy Scout survival campout. I was now forty-six years old and prone to more aches and pains. I had a middle-aged spare tire, and open water made me queasy. My previous sea kayaking excursions added up to about four hours.

The planned trip was my first assignment as a recreation planner for the Florida Fish and Wildlife Conservation Commission. Liz and I were to map and ground-truth a guide for the Big Bend Saltwater Paddling Trail. The trail had been designated by the Florida Legislature in 1996 as part of the

Greenways and Trails System, the brainchild of my good friend David Gluckman. For the past year and a half, Liz and other colleagues had worked diligently to scout remote campsites on state lands specifically for sea kayakers. One of our assignments was to double-check the distances between those campsites and take GPS readings and photos for the guide.

And perhaps prove the trail could be done by a novice.

On a gray September morning, my wife, Cyndi, dropped us off at the Lower Aucilla River Landing. Cyndi was as nervous as I was, I could tell. She knew about my inexperience, plus I would be with another woman for nine days. As she would point out later, however, if you can't trust your spouse after eighteen solid years of marriage, then you can never trust him.

Squeezing overnight gear into kayak compartments was a new experience for me, one that required ingenuity, some serious stuffing, and bungee cords and straps for those things that wouldn't fit. By the time we embarked, my long yellow boat resembled a narrow barge and seemed to move just as slowly. Liz gave me a needed lesson in paddling.

"When you stroke, push with the upper arm as much as you pull with the other and you won't get as tired," she said. "Use your upper body like a fulcrum." Good advice for the first day. If this engine ran out of gas, there was no replacement.

I tried using my foot-guided rudder and realized the pegs needed to be moved farther back so my legs could stretch all the way out. I complained to Liz. "Can you live with it for now?" she responded.

Nodding affirmatively, I glanced sideways, wondering if Liz had graduated from the same survival school as my old scoutmaster. She was about my age, but trimmer and with a more muscular definition. Her mannerisms evoked a certain toughness, an Annie Oakley with a kayak paddle. To my knowledge, Liz had never been a marine.

"We have to adjust the pedals on land," she explained, "and there's no good place to pull over."

We were nearing the Gulf, and cordgrass and needlerush extended for miles on both sides of the river in a vast wet savannah, broken by storm-battered palms. Resonant cries of hidden rails and wading birds issued from the grass, along with trilling marsh wrens. I thought of early native people who had used this river and coast. They paddled in dugout canoes crafted from huge cypress and pine trees. They didn't have foot-controlled rudders or plastic kayaks.

An alligator cruised across the river mouth, a large one. I saw only his bony eye sockets and snout before he ducked underwater. Fish—including huge longnose gar—thrashed the water's surface, startled by my boat. Occasionally a motorboat whined in the distance.

Once in the Gulf of Mexico, Liz and I headed southeast along a windswept marshy shore. Skies were still gray. Water was murky. The sea had a lonely, forbidden feel.

The tail end of Tropical Storm Henri was still churning up the Gulf—a moderate to heavy chop, as the weatherperson would say. The storm had delayed our trip by two days. At the storm's peak, an Internet weather site said the waves were rolling in at eight to ten feet high.

I tightened my life vest straps. Liz paddled up beside me. She glanced to see if my spray skirt was snapped snugly around my cockpit to keep out water. "Don't worry, this is a shallow coast," she said. "The water's not that deep. If you tip over, you can probably stand up." I nodded, trying to look cheerful.

"Do you have your whistle within reach?" she asked.

"It's in my deck bag."

"That won't do you much good if you tip over. You should attach it to your life vest." I dutifully followed her orders. Liz was a seasoned kayaker and former nurse. My survival, in part, depended upon her guidance.

I spotted the slicing fin of a bottlenose dolphin. A large sea turtle poked its head up, then quickly ducked under as we approached. Liz moved away, silhouetted against the gray, open Gulf. I dove my paddle into the water, trying to establish a rhythm, pushing and pulling simultaneously. Fulcrum, I thought. I am a fulcrum.

I flashed on a memory of fishing the Big Bend when the water was clear. A fat shark had cruised up and parked itself beneath my boat, following along as I drifted. I wondered if it was waiting for a handout, or a hand.

Suddenly, the memory of eating my first raw oyster didn't seem half bad.

2

SEMINOLE WHISPERS

Against the wind, outgoing tide, and current, we paddled up the Econfina River to our first night's camp. Our upper bodies were well exercised, so we decided to stretch our legs with a hike on one of the Econfina River State Park's overgrown nature trails. The sky was clearing, the air was warm, and the sun felt good on my face; I strolled along wearing shorts and water sandals through scrubby pinewoods and marshy hammocks. A sudden movement startled me. "Whoaa!" I exclaimed, jumping back, quickly recognizing a pygmy rattlesnake. It bravely blocked our path, refusing to budge.

Through the years, I have developed a proficient "snake jump," a semivertical backward leap often performed while uttering expletives. A bit of adrenaline can put real spring in your step; it's humorous to watch, I am told, but the maneuver has helped me avoid getting snakebit.

I was familiar with the pygmy's distinctive gray and black blotches and thin orange vertical stripe along the spine. As we scooted around it, the snake coiled back, living up to its reputation as being easily excitable. Its tiny rattle produced a low, almost imperceptible buzz.

Drop for drop, the pygmy's venom is potent, although the volume correlates with the snake's small size, thus the name *pygmy*. A pygmy's bite is generally not life-threatening for adult humans. Still, I didn't want to compare its venom firsthand with that of its bigger cousin, the diamondback.

A friend of mine was struck by a pygmy while walking a coastal shell road in sandals. He spent a painful weekend in a Port St. Joe hospital. His foot swelled, and the area around the bite turned black. We didn't want our trip to end prematurely in a similar fashion, though experience told us it was unlikely to see more than one venomous snake on an outing. We continued down the trail.

Liz saw the next two pygmy rattlesnakes. She seemed to have keener eyes for spotting camouflaged reptiles, so she took the lead. By our fourth pygmy encounter, with shadows stretching across the trail, I felt like jumping on her back and riding piggyback style. It would have made for an interesting photo, with a caption that read: "One-hundred-and-thirty-pound woman carries two-hundred-pound man along snake-infested trail."

We ceased admiring scenery; all eyes scanned the ground. By the time we spotted our fifth "easily excitable" pygmy rattlesnake, we christened the unnamed trail "The Pygmy Rattlesnake Trail." At that moment, we would have made poor ecotourism promoters: "Hike the Pygmy Rattlesnake Trail, where colorful members of the reptile kingdom will add adventure and spice to any warm weather hiking experience!"

That night, I knew Liz was the perfect wilderness partner. Some time in the wee hours, a wild animal approached her tent and started to growl. Liz growled back. The creature, most likely a wild boar, moved away.

The next morning, Liz exclaimed jokingly, "There's way too much nature out here!" What with the growling episode, scurrying raccoons, and other critters, she claimed to have taken only "little naps" during the night. I had slept fairly soundly, dreaming of otters that frolicked and played in a wild, swirling river.

We watched dawn unfold on the Econfina. A pileated woodpecker drummed, then issued its rising cry. Two chattering belted kingfishers swooped low, chasing each other across the channel. A green heron poked along a half-submerged log, almost invisible. Countless songbirds sang while the quiet wings of a red-shouldered hawk sliced through the air. I felt invigorated. No wonder Seminole and Creek Indians had fought to remain, I thought.

The Big Bend area of the 1700s and early 1800s was a refuge. Not only was it home to Muskogean peoples who had fled warfare and increased European pressure in Alabama, Georgia, and South Carolina, but untold scores of free blacks and escaped slaves formed their own villages as "maroons," or they lived with the Seminoles.

Seeking to capture escaped slaves and to punish Seminoles for raids into Georgia, General Andrew Jackson marched through the region in the spring of 1818 with more than three thousand militia and "friendly" Creeks. His forces under Lower Creek chief William McIntosh skirmished with Red Stick chief Peter McQueen's band of two hundred warriors along the Econfina. McIntosh later gave this account of the battle: "I took my warriors and went and fought him. . . . When we first began to fight them they were in a bad swamp, and fought us there for about an hour, when they ran and we followed them three miles. They fought us in all about three hours. We killed thirty-seven of them and took ninety-eight women and children and six men prisoners, and about seven hundred head of cattle, and a number of horses, with a good many hogs and some corn. We lost three killed, and have five wounded."

Jackson's forces then marched to the large Seminole and maroon villages along the lower Suwannee. At sunset, they found their prey. A small group of Black Seminoles had not yet crossed the river to safety. Muskets blazed. Highly outnumbered, black warriors fought an effective rearguard action while their families crossed the Suwannee. Finally, with darkness falling, the defenders retreated to the river and swam across. Years later, a captured combatant said they had fought as long as they could, but Jackson's forces "came too hot upon them, and they all ran to save their lives."

With the Seminoles scattered, Jackson and his men satisfied themselves with burning buildings and food supplies, capturing nine hundred head of cattle and executing two British traders accused of aiding the Seminoles.

Jackson soon returned to Tennessee—after all, he had illegally invaded Spanish territory. But it was not long before Florida was purchased by the United States and made into a territory, and then a state. Dislocated Creeks and Seminoles reclaimed their Big Bend coastal homes and vigorously fought to remain during the Second Seminole War of the late 1830s and 1840s. A fort was built on the Econfina River, along with forts on the St. Marks, Wacissa, Aucilla, Fenholloway, Steinhatchee, and Suwannee rivers, as part of the United States war effort against the Seminoles.

Several Big Bend forts saw action during the war, and one experienced a three-week siege. Hostile Seminoles also burned some of the forts, it was believed. In 1839, the commandant at Fort Andrews along the Fenholloway observed that Seminoles who camped nearby would leave every few days and return with new supplies of powder, lead, tobacco, and clothes. Throughout the war, Americans suspected that Spanish fishing boats operating out of Cuba resupplied the Seminoles, utilizing any number of remote Big Bend coves and inlets.

The Seminoles employed a highly successful form of guerrilla warfare for several years, frustrating general after general sent to subdue them. An 1836 letter from President Andrew Jackson to Florida governor and army general Richard Keith Call reveals growing anxiety over the war: "For the Lord's sake take some energetic stand, raise your people to action and energy, pursue and destroy every party of Indians that dare approach you. . . . You must act promptly and regain the military fame lost by the wretched conduct of Generals Gaines and Scott. . . . I expect you to act with energy, or you will lose your military fame."

What soldiers often feared worse than Indians were diseases. Yellow fever, malaria, dysentery, and other afflictions took a heavy toll. Troop morale was often low; desertion was common. In March 1843, Commander E. A. Hitchcock of Fort Stansbury along the St. Marks River requested discharges for twenty-eight men. By far, the most common reason given was for "being a habitual drunkard, utterly worthless as a soldier." Others were discharged for "being of feeble constitution and consumptive"; "undersized, intemperate and uncleanly in his habits"; "excessibly intemperate and worthless and undressing himself frequently"; "for murder of a fellow soldier"; "broken down physically"; "laboring under defective vision"; "insubordinate conduct and uncleanliness"; "old and unable to perform the fatigues of a soldier"; "lameness"; "being one of the greatest smugglers of whiskey"; and "broken down from the effects of the Florida service."

I can only imagine the hell of living in a small fort and blockhouse far from a friendly face, with unsanitary conditions, insufferable heat and humidity, bugs, sickness, and the crudeness and cruelty that often pervade groups of men who are cramped together for long periods of time under stressful conditions. Not surprisingly, Fort Stansbury was deactivated the same year Hitchcock filed his report. By this time, most of the Seminoles had been killed, relocated west, driven south into the Everglades, or dispersed into the backwoods.

"I have been hunted like a wolf," lamented Seminole leader Halleck Tustenugee soon after his capture, "and now I am sent away like a dog."

Liz and I took a morning paddle up the historic Econfina. We were designing the trail with an average of twelve miles between campsites so that numerous side trips could be included. We wanted to ensure ample time to

An arching sabal palm reflects on the dark waters of the lower Econfina River, one of the Big Bend's many pristine rivers.

Bleached roots of a long-dead tree along the lower Econfina River is testament to the brutal impact that storms and rising sea levels have on coastal forests.

explore the many rivers, creeks, islands, coastal towns, and historical sites along the route.

We paddled beneath canopies of cypress, gum, cedar, and huge arching live oaks, all reflecting on a mirror of tea-colored water. Tall white flowers of duck potato, radiant swamp lilies, purple spires of pickerel weed, and striking red cardinal flowers splashed the shorelines with color. Wild grape vines, called "fox grapes" by local folk, wove through overhanging branches toward the sun, dropping their purple fruit into the river.

In this upriver environment, more sheltered from storms and rising sea levels, we noticed fewer dead trees along the shore. A large variety of species was apparent, too. I spotted red bay, with its drooping clusters of brown leaves—great for seasoning soups and stews. There were also chestnut oak, live oak, and laurel oak, fragrant wax myrtle and sweetbay, grand bald cypresses, and the twisted trunks of American hornbeam. We also saw the star-shaped leaves of sweetgum, feathery cypress needles, the round fruit of buttonbush, and the smooth-barked American beech.

Mossy live oaks, festooned with resurrection fern, arched over the water. One massive live oak had spread out in various directions—up, down, and sideways—as if unsure whether to seek water or sun. At low water levels, limestone shoals can impede advancement, but on this day we were able to glide over the shoals and continue upstream.

A white-tailed deer snorted and crashed through the thick floodplain forest. I paused, watching him leave. The singing birds seemed to pause as well.

I cruised close to shore, admiring thick clusters of yaupon bushes, adorned with bright red berries. Yaupon leaves are what Creek and Seminole Indians roast and brew to make an emetic tea to be used in rituals. Historically, it was also used by native people who preceded the Creeks and Seminoles in Florida, such as the Apalachees and Timucuans. I've tried this "black drink" several times while participating in the Green Corn Ceremony and other annual Muskogee rituals. Though not Muskogee by blood, I was accepted by a ceremonial group of north Florida Muskogees more than twenty years ago.

The black drink, or *asi*, is taken after a period of fasting. One of few native plants containing caffeine, it provides a burst of clarity during rituals that take place on a cleared piece of ground covered with white sand, spreading out from a central fire. Despite its Latin name, *Ilex vomitoria*, I've never become ill from drinking *asi*, nor has it given me the slightest upset stomach. We generally take three big gulps, and on the fourth swallow, we spit out the liquid in a ritualistic act of purging. Early European observers may have witnessed this purging and assumed the liquid caused vomiting.

Before the *asi* is ingested, the drink is "doctored" by ceremonial leaders, who reverently blow into the liquid with a cane tube. A select person then gives the black drink cry, a long, drawn-out "Ya-ho-la!" Yahola was one of four legendary beings of light who visited the Muskogee people. He helped to introduce the Green Corn Ceremony as a way for the people to annually forgive all crimes short of murder, helping to ease tension and warfare among clans. He is believed to be a spiritual guardian of the ceremony. Osceola, the famous Seminole war leader, was a black drink crier for his band. His name means just that—*asi-ya-hola*, black drink singer.

Several Muskogee groups carry on ancient rituals in Florida's Big Bend, from Otter Creek to Perry to Blountstown. Many of the participants are descendents of Muskogee Creeks who either fought against the Americans during the Seminole or Red Stick Creek Wars or aided the Americans. After the wars, their ancestors either hid in the backwoods to avoid removal to Oklahoma, or they mixed with whites or blacks to better blend with the local population. For several decades, secrecy was important. Some traditions were lost, or there was a gap in participation. In today's more open environment, however, woods and waters of the Big Bend echo with the cry of "Ya-ho-la!" just as they did long ago.

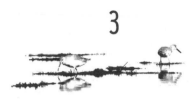

3

AIR THAT BITES

Later in the day, paddling on the open Gulf again, I had welcome visitors. A skipper butterfly landed on my deck bag and rested for a mile or so. Then a luminescent green dragonfly landed on the inside rim of my hat, perched upside down. The Muskogee people call winged creatures such as these "soul carriers." Since souls don't have wings, they need helpers like butterflies and dragonflies, the Muskogee believe. While kayaking that sunny day, soul carriers seemed an appropriate label. My spirit was soaring.

Peering toward the distant horizon, I spotted what I thought was an island and pointed it out to Liz. She shrugged. "This whole coast is about illusions," she said. "Depending on the conditions, an island that is ten miles away may look like two, and one that is two miles away may look like ten."

My "island" turned out to be a marshy peninsula. David Gluckman, an old friend who wrote a book about Florida sea kayaking, once described seeing a moving island in the distance that turned out to be a mass or "raft" of floating migratory ducks.

Miles later, as we neared a real island, Rock Island, our destination for the day, I was struck by its volcanic appearance. Black limestone jutted several feet out of the sea at low tide. Arching cabbage palms added a tropical look.

Explorations on the 20-plus-acre island revealed tidal pools brimming with crabs and small fish. I found black Indian pottery pieces, some bearing a check-stamp pattern. Armies of fiddler crabs raced across interior salt barrens while red and green dragonflies cruised the shore. We also spotted two yellow-buff female summer tanagers.

As we neared Rock Island, our destination for the day, I was struck by its volcanic appearance. Black limestone jutted several feet out of the sea at low tide.

There was a downside to our paradisiacal adventure: biting flies and, at sunset, mosquitoes and no-see-ums in great numbers. After a quickly eaten dinner of freeze-dried lasagna and surprisingly good tiramisu, we retreated to our tents. I shone my light on the tent walls and found them covered with no-see-ums—on the inside. Otherwise known as sand fleas, the minute biting flies had followed me through the door. I felt the all-too-familiar burning sensation of no-see-ums biting arms and legs. One tourist aptly described a warm evening along the Big Bend coast: "a place where the air bites."

As with mosquitoes, only the female no-see-ums bite. They feed by injecting saliva into the skin, causing blood to pool just under the surface. Hours later, a small red itchy spot often develops. Multiply this by hundreds of bites, and one can look like someone afflicted with a dreaded disease or a childhood case of measles. No-see-um larvae live in damp soils and can stay dormant for three years or longer, depending on environmental conditions—a heartening fact.

Besides the bugs, I was sweating, partly from the humidity and partly because my body had been blasted all day by intense sun. I used plenty of sunscreen, but my skin was still giving off absorbed heat. "So, why are we doing this trip in September?" I called to Liz in the other tent. The ideal time to paddle the Big Bend coast is from late October through March.

"Because we have to finish the trail guide," Liz answered.

"Oh, so we're doing the noble sacrifice for those who come after us," I responded, stripping off my clothes, splashing myself with bug repellent and flipping on my battery-operated tent fan, an ingenious invention.

"Kind of like that. Our motto can be 'if you come when it's warm, you'll wish you were someplace else.'" Again, we would have made poor ecotourism representatives.

Nature called, but I dared not hazard a trip outside the tent and incur the wrath of more no-see-ums. I used a handy ziplock bag. Liz finally decided to venture outside. After I heard her tent door unzip, she emitted muffled screams as the bugs descended. Once she returned, she exclaimed, laughing, "Wah, I wanna go home."

I thought of early native people who lived along this coast, and of how they dealt with insects. Smoldering corncobs, smoky fires, garfish oil, and wax myrtle leaves were only marginally effective, I surmised. I also flashed on the first European explorers and the hardships they suffered. One of the most wretched tales I ever read was the journal of Alvar Nuñez Cabeza de Vaca, a pre-Disney Florida tourist. Bugs were the least of his worries. In 1528, he had joined an entourage of about three hundred conquistadors on an exploration of La Florida, with the primary goal of finding gold. They were dropped off from a ship along Tampa Bay, whereupon the expedition leader, Pánfilo de Narváez, claimed the land for Spain. Then they proceeded through the Big Bend on foot and by horseback.

Since word of ruthless, uninvited guests generally travels quickly among people, the Timucuan and Apalachee Indians welcomed these Spanish tourists by shooting stone- and bone-tipped arrows that could penetrate chain mail and armor. Apalachee archers, in particular, were said to be powerful. At two hundred paces, they could send an arrow through a tree as thick as a man's leg.

Sickness also exacted a toll. A third of the men became seriously ill, and not enough horses remained to carry them out. The explorers found themselves stranded along an isolated Big Bend cove they named *Vaya de Cavallos*, the Bay of Horses, most likely Apalachee Bay near the mouth of the St. Marks River. They waited for ships that never came. After a failed attempt at desertion among the cavalry, all the men agreed to accept a common fate.

"We felt certain we would all be stricken," wrote de Vaca, "with death the one foreseeable way out; and in such a place, death seemed all the more terrible. Considering our experiences, our prospects, and various plans, we finally concluded to undertake the formidable project of constructing vessels to float away in.

"This appeared impossible, since none of us knew how to build ships, and we had no tools, iron, forge, oakum, pitch, or rigging, or any of the indispensable items, or anybody to instruct us. Worse still, we had no food to sustain workers."

Huddled together through storms and Indian attacks, eating their horses one by one, the desperate Spaniards devised a plan. They created a bellows out of deer hides and forged nails and tools out of weapons, spurs, and stirrups. They felled towering pines and shaped oars from junipers. They crafted sails from clothing, water bags from horse skin, and ropes and rigging from palmetto husks and horsehair. "Twice in this time," said de Vaca, "when some of our men went to the coves for shellfish, Indians ambushed them, killing ten men in plain sight of the camp before we could do anything about it. We found their bodies pierced all the way through, although some of them wore good armor."

In the end, the resourceful Spaniards constructed five crude sailing rafts for the 242 surviving men. "When clothing and supplies were loaded," continued de Vaca, "the sides of the barges remained hardly half a foot above water; and we were jammed too tight to move. Such is the power of necessity that we should thus hazard a turbulent sea, none of us knowing anything about navigation."

If de Vaca could have foreseen the perilous voyage ahead, one marked by great storms, thirst, hunger, Indian attacks, and more sickness, I wondered if he would have continued. Out of the many who set sail that September day, only four survivors—including de Vaca—straggled into Mexico City after journeying 6,000 miles in eight years.

Soon after de Vaca's humble arrival in Mexico City, Hernando de Soto planned for another official visit to the Big Bend. Commissioned by the Spanish King Charles to "conquer and pacify" and colonize Florida, and to find riches, he set sail with a force of six hundred heavily armed conquistadors, several priests and friars, more than two hundred horses, and a plethora of greyhounds to be used to help subjugate the Indians. Confronted with such a force, many of the village chiefs cautiously greeted the Spaniards, denied they had gold or silver, but assured them that the next village or tribe to the north had plenty. The ruse generally worked; the alluring pot of gold was always at the end of a moving rainbow that remained just out of reach.

De Soto wintered in Tallahassee, what the Apalachee called Anhaica. As many as thirty thousand Native Americans lived in the Apalachee province between the Ochlockonee and Aucilla rivers. On a side trip, de Soto's men found Narváez's earlier encampment along the Bay of Horses, one marked by horse skulls and headpieces, crosses carved in trees, logs carved into mortars, and charcoal from a forge. Knowing the fate that befell Narváez's expedition and the potential risks of their own, it must have been a grim sight.

Disappointed at having found little gold in Florida, de Soto began his infamous march through the Southeast to the Mississippi River, leaving ravaged villages and deadly disease in his wake. The Big Bend coast had served as lifeblood for generations of native people, but it was also a gateway for their destruction.

Many of the Spanish who followed de Soto were more intent on setting up missionaries and a flourishing agrarian society among the Indians now that the dream of Apalachee gold had vanished. Indian laborers were used to help raise crops for the Spanish empire. Apalachee corn and other foods were shipped along the Big Bend coast and up the Suwannee River, whereupon it was transported to St. Augustine.

Fort San Marcos de Apalachee, situated at the strategic confluence of the St. Marks and Wakulla rivers a short distance from the Gulf, was first built in 1679 by the Spanish as a way to protect their defenseless missionary priests from being kidnapped and held for ransom by pirates. The fort was constructed of logs and coated with lime to create the appearance of stone. It failed to discourage pirates, however, who raided it several times and finally set it afire.

By the turn of the next century, the fort and surrounding area became a frontier pawn in the intense tug of war between European countries trying to control Florida. The British and their Creek allies destroyed nearby missions in 1702, capturing Apalachees as slaves and driving the remaining Indians to other lands. British raids became more frequent, and in 1739, Spain finally replaced the fort's logs with limestone that was dug from beneath the saw palmetto and cut with axes while still soft. Eventually, the wet limestone became hard as granite. Better able to withstand human invaders, the fort was still no match for natural forces. The forty members of the Spanish garrison were drowned by a hurricane in 1758.

In 1800, William Augustus Bowles, a British deserter who had married a Creek woman, led four hundred Seminole and Creek Indians to capture the fort. He sought to create an Indian nation and set himself up as "King of Florida." He held the fort only five weeks before Spain reclaimed it.

During Andrew Jackson's illegal invasion of Florida in 1818, he seized the Spanish fort without a shot. He set up his own civil government and announced the capture of Florida for the United States. His actions appalled many in his own government and incurred the wrath of both Spain and Great Britain, but it made Spain realize the difficulty in maintaining control of Florida. Three years later, partly to stem the controversy, the United States purchased Florida. It marked the end of Florida's centuries-long Spanish era.

From her tent, using the glow of her headlamp, Liz began reading to me from the classic *Kon-tiki*, a South Seas seafaring adventure. While on a wilderness journey, it is useful to read about others who have experienced greater hardships. While listening, with only heat and bugs to contend with, I began to feel fortunate. The weather was calm, no shark fins had trailed my boat, we weren't depending on raw oysters or sulfur springs to survive, and there was a general lack of arrows shot in my direction. It's a lot like being told how lucky you are to *only* break a few bones in a car accident and not suffer more serious injuries.

I fell asleep by 10 p.m. Around 5 a.m., I awakened and stepped outside. A refreshing breeze greeted me, keeping no-see-ums at bay. The full moon and Mars were setting over the Gulf, a sight to behold—two celestial bodies shimmering on the water with no interference from man-made lights. This sacrificing for others could be tough, I thought.

As I sat on the island's rock face in the predawn glow, I relished the thought that several days of paddling remained. There would be more island camps, more wild rivers to explore, cool springs for swimming, and charming coastal hamlets for restocking food and water. I knew that clear water lay ahead where we could peer down into vast sea grass beds teeming with stingrays, blue crabs, horseshoe crabs, jellyfish, sea squirts, starfish, scallops, and other marine life.

At sunrise, we would continue our journey.

4

FENHOLLOWAY

We inhaled the Fenholloway River before we entered its mouth. It was an acrid odor, unnatural, characteristic of most pulp mill effluent. "I know camp food makes you fart," exclaimed Liz, "but that smell is a lot stronger."

Many of north Florida's rivers are tea-colored from tannins leaching from rotting leaves and other vegetation, creating what folks call blackwater rivers. The Fenholloway has always been a blackwater river, except its color is now less like tea and more like murky coffee. If you've been on enough rivers, you get to know which ones look healthy and which ones have an unhealthy pallor.

All of the rivers I knew while growing up near Chicago in the 1960s were tainted with sewage and/or industrial waste. It was commonplace. But heavily polluted streams are not commonplace in Florida. They are the exception, especially along the sparsely populated Big Bend coast.

Like its sister river, the pristine Econfina, the Fenholloway emerges from the San Pedro Bay swamps of northern Taylor County. As it flows past the town of Perry, population 6,847, Buckeye Technologies' Foley cellulose plant discharges up to 47 million gallons of effluent per day into the small river. The effluent, wholly derived from groundwater, is the byproduct of a complicated process that converts truckloads of pine trees into disposable diapers, incontinence pads, sanitary napkins, and other products. After winding for several more miles, the Fenholloway and its industrial burden empty into the Gulf about three miles north of Rock Island.

In 1947, the Fenholloway was designated by Florida's Legislature as the state's first and only "industrial" river. The legal designation gave Buckeye carte blanche to deposit industrial and chemical wastes into the Fenholloway River. In later years, the industrial classification was changed at the behest of environmental groups and state and federal regulatory agencies. The plant has since struggled to meet the "swimmable and fishable" standards of a Class III river, a struggle that continues.

For decades, the plant effluent contained a toxic form of dioxin known as TCDD, a probable carcinogen; Buckeye claims the plant no longer produces dioxin. The effluent is also low in dissolved oxygen, high in nutrients, and dark in color, factors that have contributed to the loss of a 10-mile-square swath of ecologically valuable sea grass at the river's mouth. Groundwater has also been polluted around the plant and along the river, forcing the company to supply its employees and affected residents with bottled water.

Interestingly, the twigs and seeds of the buckeye tree, from which the company derived its name, contain a poisonous glucoside, aesculin, for which there is no antidote if ingested. Native Americans deposited crushed buckeye into quiet pools to stupefy fish, whereupon they could easily be netted or clubbed.

The Fenholloway's role as a receptor of industrial discharge has persisted largely because Buckeye is Taylor County's main economic engine in a largely rural, otherwise impoverished area. Buckeye pumps an estimated $175 million per year into the local economy. More than six hundred people work in the plant, and numerous others are employed in related industries such as logging, tree planting, nurseries, fuel supply, chemical manufacturing, trucking, and barge operation. Employee salaries average $50,000 per year, higher than the state and national average. They lift Taylor County's economic base far above those of its neighbors.

The economic and social impact of the plant hit home for me when I attended a 2004 public hearing in Perry sponsored by the Environmental Protection Agency (EPA). The issue was whether the EPA should withdraw objections to a proposed 15-mile pipeline that would pump effluent directly into the mouth of the Fenholloway, bypassing most of the river. While six EPA representatives quietly sat on a middle school theater stage, sipping bottled water, one plant employee after another approached the podium. I sat near the front, manning a mini tape recorder.

"I was raised in this community," began Clay Bethea, a polite-speaking, clean-cut man I guessed to be in his mid- thirties. "I moved away years ago to get an education, went to Tennessee, worked for awhile. . . . I was fortunate enough to come back home and get a good job here [at Buckeye]. My job provides my family a good wage and good health care."

Clay could be any mainstream American, I thought—everyone's good neighbor—with a manicured lawn, a passel of kids, and a fistful of credit cards. He pointed out that he, like many others, purchased land and planted pine trees as an investment, trees that would one day be sold and crushed into pulp at the mill. "Some of those pine trees will be coming off as my oldest daughter enters college in eight years," he said. "It's not only big companies who own trees."

Gary Weathers, a long-term Buckeye employee, added: "This plant creates thousands of jobs. It provides low-cost health insurance coverage for thousands of people, including children, and provides millions of dollars in property tax revenue, dollars sorely needed by the state's educational system. And millions of dollars in other tax revenues—sales tax, income tax, intangibles tax, and FICA taxes. Obviously, the benefits to society exceed the environmental costs."

Gary's raspy voice had a strident tone that reminded me of listening to war veterans voice strong opinions about foreign affairs, citing God and country and advocating a "love it or leave it" approach to citizenship. It didn't pay to argue; you could only listen. "In order for our economy to survive," he continued, "somewhere in this country there must be agriculture, mining, and manufacturing. And I say, right here in Taylor County is a good place for some of that manufacturing to take place. . . . Many corporations are moving to other countries, and a good portion of the blame has been put on greedy corporations, but here we have a corporation that's doing everything it can to preserve our American jobs and keep it right here in the good old U.S.A."

The hearing was not without Buckeye's detractors. When Janice Jackson began speaking, her voice quavering with anger, I felt the pain of those dissidents in Taylor County who have been brave enough to stand up to the plant and its many employees, the local media, and local government officials. Janice was dark-haired, wiry, and feisty—a warrior—unafraid to speak her mind. "My family lived in this county since 1957," she began. "My grandfather was born in this state in 1824, so we do have a vested interest in what happens here. This company and our politicians are not good stewards. They are not good stewards because we have the Fenholloway River . . .

and the Fenholloway River is dead! We do not fish in it. We do not boat in it. We do not swim in it. We do not make iced tea with it. We do not bathe our children in it. We do not fill our fish aquariums with it. And if one of us accidentally fell into it, we would all be horrified. . . . Who is going to protect me from the effects of the Fenholloway River? Who is going to protect our children? . . . I've heard all the talk about all the money that is being spent, all the taxes and revenues that come from having the pulp mill and the Fenholloway River. I say, there is no amount of money that can buy a new river. There is no amount of money that can ensure our health, and there is no amount of money that can buy clean safe drinking water when we have none."

In defense, Buckeye officials at the hearing repeatedly cited costly plant improvements—over $64 million spent on cleanup technology since 1994, but they have long maintained that advanced pollution cleanup technology is too expensive and might force the plant to close. This position has often helped to frame the controversy as a classic "jobs versus environment" battle, inflaming passions on both sides. In 1992, tensions boiled over when environmental activist Stephanie McGuire was brutally beaten and raped by three men and thrown into the Fenholloway River. Their message to her: "Leave Buckeye alone." McGuire moved away from Taylor County.

Julie Hauserman, a writer who covered issues concerning Buckeye for more than a decade, beginning in 1991 for the *Tallahassee Democrat* and then for the *St. Petersburg Times*, experienced her share of scary moments. "I was threatened by people in person and anonymous people on the phone," she said. "They told me they'd burn my house down. They told me to watch my back. I was followed in my car basically to the county line one night after a public hearing."

Refusing to be intimidated, Julie persisted in her coverage. "When I first started covering the story, people were afraid to talk to me," she said. "They'd kind of hush if we were sitting in a restaurant and the waitress came by. It's more in the open now; people get right up and say the pollution isn't right. But it's a small crowd. Most people in Perry figure trading clean water for jobs was a good idea."

Studies during the 1990s focused on whether the Fenholloway could be rendered safe for swimming and fishing. The pipeline proposal first emerged in 1994 as one solution. The rationale was that wastewater was already flowing into the estuary and Gulf through the Fenholloway, so it would reach the Gulf either way. Plus, proponents argued that the high oxygen content and salinity of the estuary was more suitable for handling the low-oxygen saline effluent.

Detractors argued that simply relocating the effluent was not solving the problem; more advanced cleanup technology was the solution, along with a relatively low-tech measure of running the effluent through artificial wetlands. They worried that the pipeline would leave a dry Fenholloway riverbed during drought, possibly exposing dioxin-laden sediments to endangered wildlife such as wood storks. They also surmised that manatees and other marine life would be drawn to the warmer effluent during winter months. The proposal is still under review by regulatory agencies.

In recent years, Buckeye's in-plant improvements included a comprehensive wastewater treatment and recycling system, an electrostatic precipitator on a limekiln, and a new process for lightening the effluent. Replacing elemental chlorine with chlorine dioxide was a key to reducing dioxin content. The plant funded an independent study in 1998 that focused on the effects of pollution on three indicator species—the belted kingfisher, the mummichog (a small fish), and the river otter. The study concluded that treated effluent from the Buckeye plant posed little threat to fish and wildlife living in the Fenholloway.

But other research contradicts Buckeye's hired consultants. In the late 1970s, ichthyologist W. Mike Howell and his students at Samford University in Birmingham began studying small mosquitofish in the Fenholloway. They quickly identified a strange phenomenon: all of the fish, even the pregnant ones, bore a thin, elongated anal fin that males use for copulation. In other words, the physique of every female mosquitofish had become masculinized. Soon the Fenholloway gained another distinction—one of the first rivers to contain an environmental androgen that functioned like a male sex hormone. This anabolic steroid, similar to one that baseball sluggers have used to help power home runs, is believed to have arisen from the biotransformation of pollutants from the Buckeye plant. Experts are wondering how the androgen is affecting other fish and wildlife, and even humans living near the river or who consume fish from Fenholloway waters.

Buckeye argues that its improvements have made the Foley plant the best environmental performer of any North American pulp mill of its kind.

They are seeking to restore wetlands in the San Pedro Bay area to allow for a slower, more natural release of rainwater to the Fenholloway, helping to provide more river flow during periods of low rainfall. In 1998, Buckeye contracted with noted marine scientist Dr. Robert S. Livingston of Florida State University to evaluate whether plant improvements were resulting in sea grass restoration in the Gulf.

By phone I reached Michelle Curtis, wood supply manager for the Foley plant, and asked her about the study. "Because of plant improvements, the color of our effluent has been reduced by half," she said in an upbeat tone. "Sea grass is now returning to the mouth of the river, which is great. I feel very good about what is happening, but we still have work to do to restore the river to Class III standards. That is our goal. We are having lots of discussions with the EPA [United States Environmental Protection Agency] and DEP [Florida Department of Environmental Protection] about our options."

But Dr. Livingston refutes the company's interpretations of his scientific information, stating that sea grass beds only briefly rebounded during a prolonged drought period. At the 2004 EPA hearing, I watched with anticipation as the veteran scientist slowly approached the podium after numerous others had testified—mostly plant employees—for more than three hours. He appeared tired and haggard. Dark circles rimmed his eyes. When he spoke, his voice had a tone of exasperation. He confirmed that the color of the effluent had indeed improved, but by 28 percent, not 50. "It has simply not been enough to bring those sea grasses back," he concluded. "And the sea grasses are not back according to the fishes and invertebrates. There needs to be further reduction of the color discharges into the open Gulf."

Besides color, Livingston stated that another challenge is to reduce nutrients in the effluent. He warned that the Fenholloway could end up like Perdido Bay near Pensacola, which suffered an ecological collapse due to nutrient loading from a pulp mill, from sewage treatment plants, and from agricultural and urban runoff. "When you put too many nutrients in these offshore areas, it causes blooms," he said. "It's a very complex process . . . but there's a progression from the more benign blooms of diatoms into a series of toxic blooms that wipe out everything [red tide].

"Five years ago, we detected the same bloom species that started in the Perdido system were occurring in the offshore Fenholloway areas. . . . For the first time ever, we found the red tide organism. For the first time ever, it's in the Fenholloway system."

I felt stunned. Red tide was a killer. Anyone who has walked a beach littered with pungent dead fish and marine life is aware of it. I left the hearing that night knowing that "Florida's Forgotten River," as Julie Hauserman once described the Fenholloway, would continue to be an irksome challenge along an otherwise pristine Big Bend Coast.

Liz and I quickly paddled past the Fenholloway, not having the know-how to distinguish a red tide bloom from any other type of bloom, aquatic or otherwise. Still, we were amazed that crab trap buoys dotted the bay and that a lone fisherman was trying his luck in the dark waters.

After a mile or so of paddling, Liz and I escaped the smell, but I wondered about unseen pollution, and how much of it had spread out along the Gulf. Even if the quality of Buckeye's effluent has improved, it may take years or decades for sediments to be rendered harmless. Must we overlook the pollution, I wondered, in view of Buckeye's generous sale of its massive Big Bend coastal holdings to the Nature Conservancy in 1986—more than 100 square miles of coastal islands, tidal salt marsh, hardwoods hammocks, and upland pine forests? The State of Florida purchased the 60 miles of coastal frontage the following year in what was hailed as Florida's largest and most significant coastal protection measure. The land is now managed as part of the Big Bend Wildlife Management Area and provides habitat protection for more than 450 vertebrate species, including Florida black bear, manatees, bald eagles, peregrine falcons, rare salt marsh minks, and Kemp's ridley sea turtles. But can preservation offset pollution?

I thought of other thorny issues and trade-offs. What was the extent of groundwater pollution caused by the plant? What about the steady stream of air emissions? Could the cumulative environmental effects of the plant somehow correlate with Taylor County's high cancer death rates, the fifth-highest in the state? When looking at cancer, many factors must certainly be considered: race, income, health care, eating habits, smoking, and drinking, but a paper mill should be one of them.

The bottom line is that Perry is a company town. People have prospered because of the plant—they've fed their families, bought houses and trucks, purchased satellite discs, and sent their kids through college.

Millions of people have found life more convenient because of Buckeye. They've avoided the messiness of cloth diapers. They've sidestepped embarrassing moments by using incontinence pads. They've become dependent upon sanitary napkins. But I have to wonder about the price that's been paid for "progress," for convenience.

We are of the earth, traditional native people have always said, and we share the same fate. So what if a few people are sacrificed with all of those millions of pine trees? It's what a good company town must live with.

I yearn for the simpler pre-Buckeye days, when river residents and visitors were so moved by the Fenholloway's beauty they wrote songs about it. A month before the paddling trip, rummaging through dusty files at the Taylor County Historical Society, I came across a 1951 ballad called "The Old Fenholloway," in which the author extols the virtues of the river, even to the point of claiming it to be the nearest thing to the Fountain of Youth, unsurpassed by any other river in terms of beauty and life-giving properties.

During the first half of the 1900s, a resort thrived along the Fenholloway, built around a clear-flowing sulfur pool known as Hampton Springs. The resort included elaborate dining and ballrooms, sixty-three guest rooms, and a twenty-room annex for servants. A railroad spur transported visitors directly to a hotel train depot.

Like many of Florida's sulfur springs, Hampton Springs was believed to have medicinal properties, helping those suffering from rheumatism, constipation, dyspepsia, indigestion, kidney and bladder disorders, gastritis, nervousness, and skin diseases. Guests arranged to have spring water shipped to their homes for a price of six dollars for twelve half-gallon bottles.

Besides bathing in the sulfur springs, guests could gamble in a casino, go bowling, watch movies, dance, play golf and tennis, ride horses, canoe, fish, and hunt. Tour boats took them on excursions down an unspoiled Fenholloway. Guests could also drive winding, flower-bordered roads or wander landscaped gardens, complete with cascading fountains and circular pools filled with tropical fish. It must have been, like the old song says, the nearest thing to the Fountain of Youth.

By World War II, the resort had lost most of its luster, as had most of Florida's sulfur springs attractions. Visitors were lured to other places, and the springs were rumored to have lost their medicinal qualities. In 1954, the same year Buckeye opened its plant and began using the Fenholloway as its sewer, a fire broke out and reduced the ornate Hampton Springs Hotel to a smoldering pile of ashes.

The echoes of those early times are haunting in light of how the Fenholloway has been abused during the past half century. It is the victim in an economic trade-off, one that will be felt for decades to come.

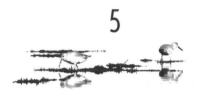

5

SPRING WARRIOR

An abandoned shrimp boat, white and barnacle-covered, loomed out of the water like a bleached dinosaur skull. I couldn't guess the reason for its abandonment along Big Spring Creek. It was now a gift for crabs, crustaceans, and small fish, a relic slowly succumbing to the elements.

The rest of Big Spring Creek resembled the myriad of other tidal creeks we had passed, snaking slowly through expansive marshlands and around lonely tree islands. The creek branched off in several directions, and Liz guided us up the right fork. "There's a small spring up here," she said. "We can swim in the spring run. That will feel good on a hot day like today. Otherwise, we'd have to paddle faster or our smell will catch up to us."

The spring water was refreshing, cool, and clear; it felt tingly on my sun-baked skin. Liz took a GPS reading and marked it on a map. "I want to include as many springs as possible for paddlers," she explained. "This is a must stop, especially when it's hot."

Lining the creek were stands of dead cabbage palms, likely killed by rising sea levels. Part of a planetary warming trend, aggravated by emissions from vehicles, factories, and power plants, a gradual shift in the distribution of native trees, plants, and wildlife is occurring. Over time, coastal tree islands will disappear, and new ones will form farther inland as the coastal forest becomes inundated. Severe storms could speed the transition by knocking out adult trees since salinity has already killed the seedlings. One report found that regeneration in some parts of the Big Bend coastal forest appears to have stopped eighty years ago due to rising sea levels.

Long-time coastal resident Shug Magnum, lamenting the loss of a small community at Adams Beach to storms and rising sea levels, observed, "The Gulf Coast along here is just getting lower and lower."

"If we continue business as usual," says Dr. Jeffrey Chanton, an environmental scientist with the Florida State University Department of Oceanography, "our current rate of fossil fuel consumption indicates that the carbon dioxide content of the air will double by 2100. This doubling will enhance the greenhouse effect and result in a one- to five-degree centigrade increase in global temperature. These temperature increases will cause sea level rise to accelerate. Best estimates are that sea level will be 400 to 500 millimeters higher by 2100, which translates to a rate of 16 to 20 inches per century. On low-relief coasts, such as the Big Bend, this could translate into hundreds of feet of shoreline loss."

According to Chanton, saltwater intrusion into groundwater, a possible change in rainfall patterns, and a greater variability in weather could also result from global warming. He maintains that global warming and the accompanying sea level rise could be slowed through the use of alternative energy sources, smaller vehicles, more energy-efficient appliances, and other conservation measures. "The earth is accustomed to slow changes, not fast ones," he says. "Slow changes allow the biosphere and earth's species time to adjust. Quick change may cause biological chaos and disrupt agricultural production."

Liz and I ended the day by inching up another stream, Spring Warrior Creek, paddling against outgoing tide, wind, and current. As I strained, I conjured up analogies to backpacking, an activity to which I was more accustomed. When the wind is at your back, it's like level walking or descending a gradual slope. Against a headwind, it's similar to climbing a slope, the severity of which could be affected by tidal changes and currents. Then there is the similarity with gear and needing to keep weight to a minimum. There are also common elements such as sore muscles, fatigue, insects, sun, and a yearning for a shower. There is the constant flip-flopping to extremes—from extreme satisfaction to hardship, from insect swarms to idyllic scenes, from calm seas to strong headwinds. It is rare to have a mediocre day.

Unlike Big Spring Creek, Spring Warrior Creek had human habitation along its shore, the tiny town of Spring Warrior. Most of the newer houses

Against outgoing tide, wind, and current, we paddled up the picturesque Spring Warrior Creek. Local residents claim it was named Spring Warrior—Warrior, for short—because Indian warriors once battled each other along its shores.

were built on tall pilings, resembling a pod of giant, square jellyfish with tentacles frozen in place. Many of the older dwellings, built at ground level, were destroyed by the No-Name Storm of 1993. The March storm surprised many along the Big Bend coast with its hurricane-force winds and tidal surge; the major thrust hit just before dawn. Most residents had never seen water rise so fast. Some were swept away while trying to retrieve car keys or shoes. Most had to swim to safety or hold onto treetops or rooftops. Hundreds of homes were destroyed. Numerous propane tanks erupted, engulfing areas with gas fumes. In all, twenty-six lives were lost, and the death toll would have been higher if it hadn't been for the heroics shown by many coastal residents in rescuing their neighbors. For people of the Big Bend Coast, it was their "Storm of the Century."

Liz and I stopped at the Spring Warrior Fish Camp, a ground-level structure damaged during the No-Name Storm and rebuilt. Owner James Pittman filled up our water jugs from freshwater he had hauled from Perry. "You don't want to drink the water around here," he said with a chuckle. "After you take a shower, you don't know whether to reach for a towel or toilet paper." The tap water had a characteristic sulfur smell common to many Florida coastal areas.

Mr. Pittman also handed us cold sodas, a welcome treat on a hot day. When we mentioned that we'd gladly pay, he just scoffed. "I'm not a wealthy man, but if I got something extra, I give it away," he said with a raspy voice that seemed on the verge of laughter. "I always have breakfast in the morning."

He had the ruddy complexion and white hair of many who have spent their lives on the sea, and the stories to go along with it.

"Rock Island!" he exclaimed when learning of our last camping spot. "Why, mosquitoes and sand fleas [no-see-ums] were invented on Rock Island!"

"And biting flies," we added.

"There was this prisoner who escaped from a road gang and somehow waded out to Rock Island. The next morning he was waving down boats. 'You tell the law to come get me,' he said. There's some things worse than being locked up," concluded Mr. Pittman.

He paused and leaned on his deck that overlooked a vast prairielike expanse of salt marsh leading to the Gulf, broken by scattered cabbage palms. The wind ruffled his hair as it does a dandelion head that has gone to seed. "I've been all over," he said wistfully, "but I wouldn't take nothing for this place."

Even though his camp has been flooded by big storms, he just cleans up and keeps on going like most of the twenty-five or so residents of Spring Warrior Creek. "The town's population never changes," he said with a twinkle in his eyes. "If a child is born in town, a man always leaves."

We made our way up the creek. The cluster of houses quickly gave way to cabbage palms, cypress, cedar, tall cattails, and blooming swamp lilies, making for a picturesque blackwater stream. Local residents claim the river was named Spring Warrior—Warrior, for short—because it was a boundary between two Indian groups, and they used to battle each other along its shores.

We set up camp on a lovely slice of public land that once belonged to a local family. On an earlier occasion, Liz had introduced me to the family's matriarch, Shug Magnum, Shug being short for Sugar. Her family still owned land in nearby Jabo Beach. With a clear voice frequently interrupted with laughter, Shug explained that cattle were once driven to the property around our campsite in order to graze on the rich coastal grasses in winter, one reason the land was relatively open. "Every winter we herded up our cows and drove them from Athena up to the mouth of the Warrior," she said. "I can remember our grandmother following up behind us with a mule and wagon with food so when we got down there we'd have something to eat."

Soon after Florida implemented a mandatory cattle-dipping program in 1923 to eliminate the Texas fever tick, Shug's family sold their cattle and deposited the money in a Perry bank. "One day my mother went in there to get some money, and the bank president said, 'I'm sorry Ms. Howard, but you don't have any money.'

"'What do you mean I don't have any money? We just put some in the bank!'

"'We're going bankrupt and don't have any more money.'

"She took her purse and hit the president of the bank. 'You son of a bitch, what do you mean I don't have any money? I know I have money!'

"She never got her money. She should have brought a bigger pocket-book."

The Perry bank likely closed during Florida's banking crisis of 1926. During a ten-day period in July, 117 banks closed in Florida and Georgia after uncontrolled depositor runs, driving Florida's economy into a depression. Depositors lost millions, bankers were ruined, and several suicides resulted. The banking industry blamed it on the collapse of Florida's land boom, one of many boom-and-bust cycles since statehood, but historian Raymond B. Vickers, after an exhaustive study of records that had been legally sealed for seventy years, concluded: "I haven't found a single bank failure that didn't involve a conscious conspiracy to defraud.... Insiders looted the banks they pledged to protect. They tried to get rich by wildly speculating with depositors' money, and when their schemes failed so did their banks."

Vickers added that problems with the industry have persisted. "Bankers and regulators, bound by a code of secrecy, have created an invisible regulatory system within the government," he wrote. "It is a system of covert regulators with imperialistic powers but without public accountability."

The wrath of Shug's mother may have been well placed, especially if it had been directed at government regulators and politicians as well.

In happier times, the east bank of Spring Warrior was a favorite Thanksgiving gathering place for Shug's family. "We'd snore [gather] worms and take them down there and catch shellcrackers, redbreast, and catfish," she said. "We'd also hunt squirrel and duck. We never bought anything back then except sugar, flour, coffee, and grits."

Shug alluded to a long-standing feud between area families that erupted over open-range cattle in the late 1800s, a Florida version of the Hatfields and McCoys. Several gunfights and ambushes occurred. "People had too many cows," she explained. "That's what caused some of the problems, 'cause your cows would go down and get on somebody else's property, and that man's cows would come up and get on your property." The conflict turned Taylor County into the "Wild West," she said.

The two main families involved in the dispute, the Towleses and the Brannens, moved into Taylor County soon after the Civil War and settled just south of the Fenholloway near Spring Warrior. They logged cedar and raised cattle.

Tension grew over missing cattle and the claiming of unmarked calves, but the tale doesn't get juicy until Tom Brannen's young, pretty, and recently married sister, Jincy Lanier, began having an affair with Jim Towles. The affair became public, and Tom warned Jim to stop seeing his sister. Evidently, Jim wasn't a man to be bullied, especially by a Brannen. He allegedly ordered his henchman, Brad Hampton, a mulatto half brother, to shoot Tom Brannen and his close friend, Bunk Padgett. Only Padgett was killed; the bullet meant for Tom went astray. Tom Brannen then murdered Brad Hampton. He told someone afterward how Hampton had looked when he died, flailing in the dirt while trying to grab for his gun.

The murders set off an 1890s range war in which gunmen were said to be hired by both sides. Most killing was done by ambush. Cautious residents kept their yards free of vegetation and swept clean every night in order to spot suspicious tracks in the morning, human or snake. The county census between 1880 and 1900 may reflect the impact the feud had on the total population—it decreased by 157.

A warrant was issued for Tom Brannen's arrest for the murder of Brad Hampton, but he hid with family and friends and often camped in Tide Swamp, near the coast between present-day Keaton Beach and Steinhatchee. After years on the run, a sheriff's posse eventually gunned him down in 1899 while he answered a call of nature, but the violence between the Towleses and the Brannens continued into the next century and ensnared other families and individuals. The county sheriff and his deputy were among the fatalities reported.

At one point, Jim Towles and George Brannen were both hunting hogs in the same vicinity when a sudden thunderstorm struck. They both sought shelter in a deserted shack and found themselves face to face. According to legend, George ventured an apology, but Jim replied, "The more you stir the old shit, the more it stinks."

In 1969, Gwen Faulkner, then a Florida State University graduate student in English, interviewed several Taylor County residents about the feud, people who had lived through it as children or young adults. Most were cautious about revealing information, one man saying, "there's lotsa people in Taylor County who ain't fergot." Another proclaimed, "The past is dead, let it lie."

Bill Towles, son of Jim Towles, said only this, "What happened to Brannen was what shoulda happened."

Walter Wright of Perry was more talkative. He remembered both Tom Brannen and Jim Towles. Of Jim, he said, "He was a medium-sized man. He had pretty heavy shoulders on him. . . . You could trust him, in a way. Some things he'd keep and some he wouldn't. . . . He'd do anything in the world for you, but he wanted two-folds back."

He had more to tell about Tom Brannen: "He was a slim man, a medium-sized man, only he was pretty tall. High cheekbones. Indian in him. He was pleasant to be around. I remember him well. He'd set down at my Daddy's table with his rifle laying cross his lap. Eat at my Daddy's table. That was about the time the Governor issued that warrant for his arrest. It shouldn't have made him mad. He knew he was guilty. They'd been shooting each other down in that swamp in the Cedar Days. Tom had him a camp down in there and there was a tall cabbage [palm] standing there and he'd nailed slats up it and he'd go up there and lookout to the coast side. A bunch of 'em went right up to that camp. Now he had shootin-holes in the sides of that camp and I heard tell he killed the bunch of 'em."

At our Spring Warrior camp, it was difficult to imagine the violence that took place not that long ago, times when a man had to be cautious about passing palmetto thickets or stepping into firelight. The only cries were those of barred owls echoing across moonlit water. From inside my tent, I could hear the soothing murmur of Spring Warrior, winding toward the Gulf. Soon my dreams flowed out to join her.

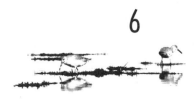

6

SHITTY BILL

Not far from our Spring Warrior camp is home of one of the Big Bend Coast's most colorful characters, Billy Sullivan, a.k.a. Shitty Bill. Liz took me to meet him. In scouting the trail and campsites, Liz did more than simply explore state-owned lands and waterways; she came to know key people in each area, people who could support the trail and its paddlers. Shitty Bill was one.

When we entered his small spit of land jutting into salt marsh, Billy grinned and gave Liz a hug, careful not to spill his can of beer. He was stocky, clad in loose-fitting hunter fatigues, and when he spoke, his eyes widened and his voice easily became animated. He immediately guided us to his crow's-nest deck atop his small house, as if that were the polite thing to do for visitors. From the deck, we gazed out over a panorama of marsh and water and could easily see the southeastern arc of the coastline—Florida's Big Bend.

"See that peninsula," Billy said, pointing to where we were looking. "At the very end, where the trees make the shape of a B-29—see, you can make out the tail wing, that's where I was born and raised. That's Jug Island."

With youthful enthusiasm—not what you normally expect from a fifty-nine-year-old—Billy described what it was like to grow up along the coast in the late 1940s and early 1950s. "As soon as the school bus dropped us off on Friday, my brothers and I would be off in the woods along the coast. We'd catch fish, gig frogs, cut us some swamp cabbage, and cook everything we caught or gathered in a big coffee can. Our coffee was just some boiled acorn hulls. If it growed and it wasn't poison, we ate it or we tried it. At

"I bought this house and 20 acres for twenty thousand dollars," says Billy Sullivan, a.k.a. Shitty Bill. "It's worth about eight million now, but I won't sell it. What is it to have a lot of money? You'd never find another place like this."

night, we'd rake up the leaves and cover ourselves up. On Sunday, our parents would gather us up. They'd make us ride in the back of their truck 'cause we stunk so bad."

Billy's family, like other families in the area, raised hogs. "We marked their ears, cut their tails off, and let them go in the woods. We'd drive through the woods with a bucket of corn once a week. We'd drive through blowing that horn and they'd all meet us. They'd know where to meet us. We'd count 'em and see which ones needed to be culled or whatever, which ones had pigs, and if you killed another man's hogs, you'd have to take him half the meat. Back then a hungry man didn't go without.

"They [hogs] kept me up a tree many a day. It was either climb that tree or kill that hog, and I'd rather climb that tree than get a beating, 'cause Aunt Hettie would whup us if we shot one of her hogs. Aunt Hettie run Jug Is-

Billy Sullivan stands atop his deck overlooking a marshy wilderness and a sign that pro-claims his nickname. Deer racks nailed to a PVC post attest to his hunting prowess.

land. She was mayor, marshal, and judge of Jug Island. She was tough. Aunt Hettie Hogan. She had a sponge boat fleet. Oh, them Greeks were something else. They'd get drunk all the time, and finally she got so aggravated she burned every one of them boats. Put them out of business. If you go to Jug Island right now, you'd see the old hulls laying there when the tide goes out.

"Her husband named that island. He come in on a boat and he found a jug up under a tree, I imagine a whiskey jug, and called it Jug Island. We were raised there."

From his crow's nest, seeing in all directions, it was easy to visualize the events Billy described. I felt privileged to be with someone who could point out his place of birth, the woods where he roamed, and the places he fished. It was equally special to be with someone who was not tempted by money to sell out. "About eight years ago, before we bought this place, we were living in our house in Perry. My son, Joe, came home one day after fishing with a friend. His friend told Joe, 'I'd like to sell this place to someone who would enjoy it, and I know your family will.' So Joe come home and told me, and I said, 'Son, we can't afford nothing like that.' Joe said, 'He told me to tell you to call him.' I did. Man, I hit the bank and mortgaged my house in Perry. I bought this house and twenty acres for twenty thousand dollars. It's worth about eight million now, but I won't sell it. What is it to have a lot of money? You'd never find another place like this. Life is too short to not do what you enjoy, even if you make a bit less money. I mean, what would you do if you made more money? You'd just spend it."

Billy griped about rising property values and their associated taxes, boosted by increased development pressure in the area. One plan calls for a massive gated community, golf course, and marina a few miles away, near Dekle Beach. "There's going to be a lot more boats out there fishing," he lamented. It is one of the first inroads of South Florida–style development along the Big Bend coast.

Billy pointed in the northwest direction, changing the subject. "See the island off to the left. All of this was saltworks. During the Confederacy, they let them out of fighting to come and make salt. They had a quota. Many came from Georgia. The Union gunboats would come along here and shell them. Come on, I'll show you." We climbed down from the crow's nest. Billy seemed to take pride in the crooked stairwell. "I built that near the end of the day," he said. "I had had a few beers by then."

The Confederate saltworks are marked by trees growing atop waist-high piles of bricks and stones. This was where furnaces had been built to heat up giant iron kettles filled with seawater. Here Liz examines rubble at one pile near Adams Beach.

We hopped in Billy's pickup and drove on salt barrens just inside the high marsh, dodging large black limestone boulders. "It's like lava rock," Billy exclaimed. "All underneath the sand here is solid rock. In one spot, the rocks seem to make a perfect circle."

We parked and walked to a cluster of teardrop-shaped cedars dominated by a lone cabbage palm. The trees grew atop a waist-high pile of bricks and stones. This was where a furnace had been built to heat up a giant iron kettle filled with seawater. In the distance, we could see similar mounds rising out of the marsh.

Before our kayaking trip, I had researched the saltworks and was thrilled to see the remnants. One reference claimed that this stretch of coast southwest of Spring Warrior Creek harbored the largest concentration of saltworks in the Confederacy, producing about 1,500 bushels of salt a day at its peak. The South depended on huge quantities of salt to cure meat for the Confederate army. With the Union navy blockading salt imports from England and other nations, demand for salt rose exponentially. In 1861, the Confederacy could buy salt for between seventy-five cents and three dollars a bushel. By 1864, the price had risen to $12.50 a bushel at the government saltworks, but enormous prices could be obtained when salt was shipped inland. A rush to buy salt marshes ensued, and the state placed an injunction on any sale of marshes in the public domain.

Tallahassee native Susan Bradford Eppes described a salt-making operation in her Civil War diary, a fascinating 1926 book entitled *Through Some Eventful Years*:

> October 27th, 1863.—We went to the salt works today. . . . It is a rather dangerous place to work, for the Yankee gunboats can get very near the coast and they may try shelling the works.
>
> . . . The great big sugar kettles are filled full of water and fires made beneath the kettles. They are a long time heating up and then they boil merrily. Ben and Tup and Sam keep the fires going, for they must not cool down the least little bit. A white foam comes at first and then the dirtiest scum you ever saw bubbles and dances over the surface, as the water boils away it seems to get thicker and thicker, at last only a wet mass of what looks like sand remains. This they spread on smooth oaken planks to dry.

The shallow coast prevented large Union ships from approaching too close, but in 1864, small boats launched from the USS *Tahoma* carried Union soldiers to strategic spots along the shore. They proceeded to destroy the Taylor County saltworks. Since most of Florida's Confederate troops were in the field fighting major battles farther north, the saltworks were not defended. The tally of damage reveals the magnitude of the operations: "390 large kettles, 52 sheet-iron boilers with an average capacity of 900 gallons, 170 masonry furnaces, 150 pumps, wells, and aqueducts, 55 store houses, 165 houses and shanties, and 60 sheds and stables."

Helping the Union on raids of the saltworks and in blockading ports and rivers were scores of northern sympathizers. Many were Confederate deserters from various states who had found refuge along the coastal rivers. They often camped under the watchful eye of Union boats. Slaves sometimes obtained freedom by swimming or rowing out to the blockade boats.

Perhaps taking a cue from Seminole Indians two decades before, bands of deserters began a type of guerrilla war against the Confederacy. In response, Brigadier-General William M. Gardner set an ultimatum: unless Confederate deserters rejoined the army, their families "will be sent into the interior, their property destroyed, and all the cattle, horses, and hogs will be driven away or shot."

Gardner was true to his word. In March 1864, every house belonging to a deserter along the Econfina and Fenholloway rivers was destroyed. At one home, two thousand rounds of ammunition and numerous barrels of flour from the U.S. Subsistence Department were discovered, along with a document that described a regiment of thirty-five men who called themselves "the Independent Union Raiders of Taylor County, Fla."

In her journal, Susan Bradford Eppes describes the deserters, and the actions that were taken:

> An enemy we had with whom we were unable to cope, *the diabolical deserter*. From some of the counties, lying adjacent to the waters of the Gulf of Mexico, soldiers had been conscripted and the Confederate Government did not realize that "a man who is forced is a man to be feared." The price they paid for this knowledge was a terrible one. The women of this land of deserters would go on visits to their kinsfolk and friends in the interior. They would "spy out the land," prolonging their visits until some news of military movements could be gained, then back home they went to tell what they had found out to these deserters, who lost no time in rowing a small boat out to the blockader and proudly telling the news they had gleaned.

Eppes described nine double-pen log houses being built just outside of Tallahassee, and wondered about their purpose. She soon learned that wagons were sent to Big Bend coastal rivers, whereupon the deserters' families were packed up along with their belongings. "The torch was applied and the troops remained until each filthy cabin was in ashes," Eppes wrote. "Ere midnight of that day the nine double houses were filled and an additional tent was pitched to accommodate the overflow."

Led by Billy, Liz and I poked into some of the small tree islands created by the saltworks rubble. "Better watch it walking in there," Billy cautioned. "That's the highest ground around here. That's where the rattlers hang out."

We nodded, knowing the truth of his words. While clearing a trail to a coastal campsite, I had nearly stepped on a diamondback in dense needle-rush grass, a hefty four-footer. He had only hissed a warning, never once rattling.

Billy excitedly pointed out fresh deer and hog tracks. "This is where they come to get away from the hunters," he said. "I've seen some boars out here that look like damn cows." Although Billy was a hunter himself, shooting

A crumbling sidewalk juts out toward the marsh along the undeveloped Bonita Beach. Built in the 1920s, the owner took photos of the sidewalk and mailed them to "friends" up North, advertising beachfront property.

several deer a year, he rarely kills deer on his property. "This place is like a sanctuary," he said with a tone of reverence.

Billy showed us another curious relic of the past, a crumbling sidewalk about a hundred yards long built across the marsh. "That's a city subdivision right there," he said. "It's on the plat, Bonita Beach. In 1924 or '26, this guy came from up North and platted it out. It's still active on the books."

According to an old newspaper clipping I had found, the sidewalk was a means to make a profit from waterlogged property. The owner took photos of the sidewalk and mailed them to "friends" up North, advertising beachfront property. He failed to mention that Bonita Beach was not the type of white-sand beach most would-be investors had in mind. It was shallow and marshy, with little dry land at high tide. In other words, the sidewalk was a front for a classic Florida land scam. The owner took his money and returned to Ohio, leaving the sidewalk to the scurrying fiddler crabs and sun-loving lizards.

We drove back to Billy's small one-room home to view his collection of rattlesnake buttons, raccoon penises, turkey beards, and projectile points. They hung from fishing lines in front of the windows like strange holiday ornaments. I had seen people in the Southwest hang green and red peppers in a similar manner.

Billy's brown-haired wife stayed glued to the computer, playing an online slot machine. Occasionally, she'd glance up at a football game on television. "Oh, that pass was way overthrown," she moaned at one point, then redirected her attention to the slot machine.

"I'd better be careful," whispered Billy, "or she'll want me to take her back to Biloxi. Already took her a couple of weeks ago."

Once we were outside again, standing beneath a vertical row of deer racks tacked to a PVC post, beside a sign that read, "Shitty Bill's Fish Camp," curiosity got the best of me. "So, how come they call you Shitty Bill?"

Billy gave me his boyish grin. "When I bought this place, I just was enjoying myself so much down here that my wife come down from Perry and said, 'Billy, when you coming home?' I said, 'Hell, I am home.' So, we worked out a deal. If she wants good cooking, she comes see me. If I want good loving, I'd go see her. You know what, I got shit on again. I got too old for the good loving, and she eats every day! And I had to cook for her, you hear? I got the wrong end of the stick. That's why they call me Shitty Bill." He laughed his effortless laugh. It was easy to feel comfortable around Shitty Bill.

I mentioned that we were meeting all kinds of friendly people along the coast. Billy didn't seem surprised. "Coastal people are friendly folks," he said, as if they were a separate breed. I wondered if it was the salt air and panoramic views, or whether it was because the sea could be generous at times, providing much bounty; maybe one felt obligated to share.

Billy pointed down his driveway. "They say you'll find a pot of gold if you follow a rainbow to the end. Well, one day this rainbow come from Adams Beach, circled and made its curve, and touched down right beside my gate. It just lit up the trees with all the colors. It was real purty."

Maybe that's why Shitty Bill won't sell out. While many people are scrambling to find that elusive fortune, Billy's fortune found him.

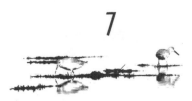

7

"A LEWIS CARROLL ENVIRONMENT"

Paddling past Jug Island, we hoped to see signs commemorating the birth-place of Shitty Bill, but there was only a large white house and a long dock covered with shorebirds. The noisy gulls and sandpipers either flew over-head or ran along the dock as we passed underneath.

Keaton Beach was a welcome spot for a long lunch break. A county park at the end of a peninsula had cold showers, and Liz and I enjoyed fried grouper sandwiches, fries, fried okra, and giant glasses of iced tea at a nearby restaurant. Ketchup rounded out the deep-fried feast.

"Where can we buy some fresh vegetables?" Liz asked Marcia, a friendly "retired" woman who said she worked at the restaurant three days a week. After days of freeze-dried food, we were dreaming of fresh broccoli, salad greens, and carrots.

"Well, there's a place about a mile and a half down the road. I get off in ten minutes. I can take you there."

We took her up on the kind offer.

Keaton Beach has one main road, lined with tightly packed houses, bait shops, and marinas, many of them rebuilt since the No-Name Storm of 1993. "I love living here," Marcia said.

"What do you do when you're not working at the restaurant?" I asked, curious about leisure activities in Keaton Beach that didn't involve baiting a hook.

"I make mosaics," Marcia replied proudly. She was excited to learn about the paddling trail and the ecotourism revenue it might generate.

Our "fresh" vegetables turned out to be frozen corn on the cob, but experiencing Marcia's act of kindness toward two strangers made the drive worthwhile. She reminded me of generous people I had met in towns along the Appalachian Trail, which I had hiked in 1975 at age eighteen. Would towns such as Keaton Beach be friendly "trail towns" for paddlers? It was off to a good start. We hoped to receive positive feedback from future travelers.

Leaving town, an elderly man greeted us. "Oh, I love to kayak," he said, scanning our boats. "I wish I could go with you, but I'm eighty-two years old."

"Go get your boat and come along," responded Liz. The man smiled appreciatively and wished us luck.

We had an easy paddle to Sponge Point, where we camped beneath huge live oaks and mature cedars. For evening entertainment, we watched ospreys dive into a sunset-colored Gulf. Long-necked egrets poked into calm water, and great blue herons loudly croaked as they lumbered past. There were few biting insects thanks to squadrons of dragonflies hovering overhead. They sometimes maneuvered close to snatch away bugs, serving as personal bug zappers. "This is a magical spot," Liz whispered. Any loud talking would have somehow seemed sacrilegious.

We sat and talked quietly until 10 p.m., a record. It was perfect camping weather. We listened for wild hogs since we had seen ample evidence of their rooting along shore. Their frequently used trails led through a wide stretch of marsh to the mainland.

Wild pigs were first brought to Florida by the earliest Spanish explorers, and they have gone forth and multiplied in biblical proportions. If hunting pressure is increased, they often compensate by producing larger litters, depending on food supply. At Sponge Point, we assumed they were rooting up fiddler crabs or searching for plant tubers or the eggs of marine animals. They are opportunistic feeders.

The full moon rose and cast everything in silvery light. If it were spring, I would have expected to see a multitude of horseshoe crabs crawling onto the sandy beach. I once visited Mashes Sands near the mouth of the Ochlockonee River to witness a mass nesting aggregation of horseshoe crabs. Under moonlight, their brown dome-shaped carapaces collectively resembled a strange geologic formation or a quivering road of helmet-sized cobblestones.

When a crab flipped over, it used its harmless spikelike tail to right itself. I picked up one of the crabs near my feet, knowing it could not bite, pinch,

We had an easy paddle to Sponge Point, where we camped beneath huge live oaks and mature cedars. Unfortunately, we lodged our kayaks on a long ridge of dead ocean plant material known as tidal wrack, a popular breeding ground for insects and arthropods. Hundreds of tiny bugs leaped into our cockpits and were impossible to remove.

or poke me. With a flashlight, I tried to find its nine eyes, the two main ones being on either side of the shell. Horseshoe crab eyes have helped scientists understand the mechanisms of vision. I felt the creature's armored shell, made up of chitin, a substance used to make contact lenses, skin creams, and hairsprays. Chitin can also shorten the healing time of burns and wounds when it is used for sutures, skin grafts, and dressings.

Hidden from my view was the horseshoe crab's valuable blood, which turns blue when exposed to air. The blood contains a component called limulus amoebocyte lysate, otherwise known as LAL. LAL coagulates in the presence of small amounts of bacterial by-products called endotoxins, thus making it the most effective known substance in testing for bacterial contamination in commercial drugs and medical equipment. A liter of LAL will fetch thousands of dollars. Fortunately, a small amount of the vital substance can be extracted without harming the crab. Once ground up for fertilizer and animal feed, the ancient horseshoe crab is now saving human lives.

More closely related to land spiders than true crabs, horseshoe crabs have been drawn to beaches during the full or new moons for more than 350 million years. Males often intercept females on their way to beaches and, using specialized front claws, attach themselves and crawl onto the beach together. While the larger female lays eggs in the sand, the male fertilizes them. One female can lay as many as eighty thousand eggs in a season.

Horseshoe crab eggs are a major food source for migratory birds. The young crabs that do survive will crawl into the water and remain on the bottoms of intertidal flats for nine to eleven years before returning to the beach to nest. They can live up to twenty years. Another beach nester, the loggerhead sea turtle, often feeds on horseshoe crabs.

Primarily along the East Coast, the American eel and whelk fisheries have used millions of horseshoe crabs for bait, prompting regulations in most coastal states. Harvesting of horseshoe crabs, coupled with the building of seawalls and other development, have contributed to an overall decline in horseshoe crab abundance, impacting shorebird species that feed on their eggs. Wild shores such as Sponge Point are vital to their survival.

Sponge Point likely received its name from the once-popular sponge-fishing industry. Beginning in the late 1800s, sponge fishermen harvested high-quality sponges off the Big Bend coast. Early spongers were most often from the Keys, the Bahamas, Cuba, or the Greek Islands (based in Tarpon Springs).

Shallow-water spongers were called "hookers" because they hooked sponges with long poles rather than diving off a boat. They worked from dinghies manned by two men: an oarsman and a hooker. Deep-water spongers used larger boats and crews and supported divers who utilized diving bells and air hoses. Sponge boats worked year-round, with workers signing on for six-month stints. In warm months, they worked the Big Bend area; in winter months, they'd head to south Florida and the Everglades. Because the sponge business was so lucrative in the first half of the twentieth century, Tarpon Springs largely avoided the financial sting of the Great Depression.

In the mid-1940s, a massive outbreak of red tide that lingered for years killed or damaged most Gulf sponges. This natural blight, combined with an influx of synthetic sponges on the market, spelled disaster for the sponge industry. Most spongers were forced to find other lines of work. Many moved to northern states to toil in steel mills or to become high-structure painters.

Today, spongers can occasionally be found off the Big Bend coast, generally diving in waters less than 60 feet deep. Most still hail from Tarpon Springs. Modern divers usually sport a mask, wetsuit, weighted shoes and belt (depending on depth), and use a hose attached to an air compressor that runs off an engine on the boat. The sponges off the Big Bend coast are generally of high quality, having a dense skeletal structure. The most prized sponges in the world are said to be deep-water Gulf sponges known as "Florida Rock Island wool."

Two friends of mine, Bob and Jamie Hayes of Tallahassee, sponged for a ten-year period. "I met Jamie in 1973 when I was working for the phone company," said Bob. "We met a Turkish man named Ali who was living with the Greeks in Tarpon Springs. I was twenty-three or twenty-four and looking for anything adventurous. When he showed us sponging, I quit the phone company the next week, and we signed on with a sponge boat. A few months later, the owner of one boat drowned, and we bought his boat in 1974."

Bob smiled when he recalled the moment they first embarked from Tarpon Springs in their new sponge boat, a young couple in love along with a Turkish man. "The Greeks wouldn't say good luck," he said. "They'd say good-bye. They were also superstitious because a guy drowned off that boat."

To the surprise of many in Tarpon Springs, Jamie and Bob survived their first season and soon gained a reputation for being hard-working and for providing high-quality, clean sponges. When Bob dove, he normally used a 300-foot air hose, mask, wetsuit, and weighted shoes and belt. "I liked being in 15 to 20 feet of water," said Bob. "In shallow water like that, you can stay down longer and take off, and hopefully run into a piece of bottom that hasn't been worked for a while. It's basically like gold hunting. If you fall into it, it's a wonderful feeling."

Bob tried to describe underwater environments filled with multicolored sponges, some a fiery-orange, along with deep-red sea fans, huge boulders of brain coral, rocks covered with white and purple algae and bryozoans, brown-purple octopuses, pink spiny sea urchins, and yellow starfish. "I had a chance to see some amazing, psychedelic types of bottom, just wild, with

Early in the morning at Sponge Point near Keaton Beach, we awakened to see the moon setting while the sun was rising at our backs. I asked Liz to pose for a shot in her kayak, a tough request since she hadn't had her coffee.

sponges and corals of all shapes and sizes and colors. It was like a Lewis Carroll environment."

Jack Rudloe, in his book *The Living Dock*, had a similar reaction when describing the live bottoms off the Big Bend: "No treasure chests brimming with rubies and sapphires, diamonds and emeralds, or gold and silver could compare with it.... I felt that I was looking at Pharaoh's treasures."

Bob pointed out that he often had an opposite reaction when the water was murky, and the many underwater formations appeared as dark ominous blobs.

Jamie's job on the boat was lifeline tender, cook, and deckhand. "I only dove for sponge in the Keys because it was clear and shallow," she said. "Sometimes we could free dive, depending on the depth and current." Bob and Jamie sponged from Carrabelle to Tarpon Springs and south to the Keys and Bahamas. "We did most of our harvesting south of the St. Marks,

Lush underwater sea grass meadows blanket nearly the entire broad, shallow shelf of the Big Bend coast, one reason why much of the coastline was purchased by the State of Florida.

Aucilla, and Econfina river areas," said Jamie. "The Fenholloway area was devoid of sponge because of the paper mill."

Bob and Jamie were married on a sponge boat in 1975, but when they started a family a few years later, Bob began to work construction jobs on land. "The fisherman's life isn't a vocation; it's a lifestyle." said Bob. "It's a wonderful feeling if you don't have a lot to worry about on shore, because you're out in the Gulf for ten or twenty days at a time. You can't have too much of a family life. When you're young and crazy, it's easier."

With their two children now grown up, Bob and Jamie recently purchased a 25-foot sailboat. "We hope to sail around Cuba," said Bob, excitement growing in his voice. "And we might ease back into the sponge business."

In the morning, Liz and I stood on Sponge Point's marshy shore during the one morning a month when the sun rises while the full moon sets—two celestial bodies seeming to mirror each other.

Another magical part of the morning was the water clarity. The effects of Tropical Storm Henri were finally diminishing. While paddling, we could see the shallow sea grass beds below and a multitude of scallop shells, small rays, blue crabs, horseshoe crabs, and bulbous-looking jellyfish. A small shark thrashed its way into the shallows, hunting baitfish. A school of silvery trout churned the water in a feeding frenzy. "It's like paddling through a giant aquarium," exclaimed Liz. We were enjoying the expanded view of not only the sky and views around us but also the world below.

Lush underwater sea grass meadows blanket nearly the entire broad, shallow shelf of the Big Bend coast. The Big Bend coast joins Florida Bay as having two of the most extensive sea grass beds in North America, one reason why much of the coastline was purchased by the State of Florida.

Sea grass beds are vital to the marine environment and Florida's economy. A wide range of commercially and recreationally important species—including red drum, spotted sea trout, sea bass, and mullet—use these meadows as nurseries, feeding grounds, and refuges from predation. In fact, 70 percent of Florida's marine recreational fish depend upon sea grass communities at some time in their lives.

Bay scallops, crabs, many types of shrimp, and other commercially viable species also live in sea grass beds, along with starfish, seahorses, and other intriguing creatures. A host of wading birds feed in sea grass beds at low tide.

Two of the most common underwater grasses are turtle grass and manatee grass, so named for the sea turtles and manatees that graze on them. Shoal grass is another species common in Florida waters.

My neighbor Paul and I often fish the Big Bend's sea grass beds, what fishermen commonly refer to as "the flats." The beds are often interspersed with open patches of sand and occasional oyster bars, making for an underwater quilt of green, tan, and black. We usually launch a canoe at some remote landing, wind through a maze of tidal creeks, and paddle like crazy for almost two miles in open water before reaching a water depth of six feet at high tide.

On one occasion, we became completely fogged in offshore and learned, to our chagrin, that we had forgotten a compass. Fortunately the water was clear, and we found our way back to shore by looking at sea grass. The incoming tidal flow had caused each blade to point north, toward shore—convenient underwater trail markers. We came away with a new appreciation for sea grass.

Sea grasses are fascinating in their own right. They are the only flowering plants that live their entire lives in seawater. They help to stabilize the sea

I often fish along the Big Bend coast with my neighbor Paul Force. Here Paul poses with a nice redfish caught along the lower Aucilla River.

bottom, contribute to water clarity, and soften the blow of storms. Sea grasses filter pollutants, absorb nitrogen from the water, and release vital oxygen. However, contaminated runoff from residential, industrial, and agricultural sources can produce algae blooms that block sunlight and wipe out sea grasses. These blooms, coupled with careless boating, dredge-and-fill projects, and coastal construction, have destroyed sea grass beds in numerous areas of Florida. In response, many communities, such as those along Tampa Bay, are working hard to reduce pollutants reaching coastal waters, and some are even growing and planting sea grasses, achieving modest gains.

We stepped out of our boats in the shallow water at Long Grassy Point for a bathroom break, dodging several hat-sized stingrays that scooted across the sandy bottom. We quickly jumped back into our boats. All of this sea life could be disconcerting when out of the boat. We moved offshore, and once again we were enjoying the vast aquarium of the Gulf of Mexico, sea grasses arching over with the rising tide.

8

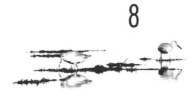

EARLY PEOPLES

In paddling along an unspoiled coast, with each new cove adorned with colorful wading birds, it was easy to picture early native people in dugout canoes, either on trade journeys, fishing, or simply moving from one camp to the next, as we were.

William Bartram wrote of Native Americans traveling by dugouts during his travels through Florida in 1773. He stayed at the Indian town of Tala-hasochte, along the Suwannee near Manatee Springs, about 30 miles from the Gulf.

> These Indians have large handsome canoes, which they form out of the trunks of Cypress trees (Cupressus disticha), some of them commodi-ous enough to accommodate twenty or thirty warriors. In these large canoes they descend the river on trading and hunting expeditions to the sea coast, neighboring islands and keys, quite to the point of Flor-ida, and sometimes cross the gulph, extending their navigations to the Bahama islands and even to Cuba: a crew of the adventurers had just arrived, having returned from Cuba but a few days before our arrival, with a cargo of spirituous liquors, Coffee, Sugar, and Tobacco. One of them politely presented me with a choice piece of Tobacco, which he told me he had received from the governor of Cuba.
>
> They deal in the way of barter, carrying with them deer-skins, furs, dry fish, bees-wax, honey, bear's oil, and some other articles.

As the afternoon heat rose, we became increasingly hot, tired, and smelly. A fungus grew between my toes from constant dampness, a condition early travelers surely experienced. At Liz's suggestion, we began to recount the many adjectives that described our condition—fetid, repulsive, festering, putrid, gangrenous, malodorous.

As an added bonus, insects plagued us. The night before, we had lodged our kayaks on a long ridge of dead ocean plant material known as tidal wrack, a popular breeding ground for insects and arthropods. Hundreds of tiny bugs had leaped into our cockpits and were impossible to remove. They looked like an odd sort of jumping shrimp. The bugs were bothersome, crawling on our legs. Biting flies that flew into the cockpits were worse. We realized the need to cover cockpits with spray skirts during the day and night since neither of us was a saltwater entomologist in search of specimens. I'd venture that several new species of insects might be discovered along the Big Bend coast during warm weather.

"So why are we doing this trip in early September?" I asked Liz for the umpteenth time.

"Because we are idiots!" she responded with a grin. "And we're working."

We took a break at remote Dallus Creek Landing, part of the Tide Swamp Unit of the Big Bend Wildlife Management Area. An unpaved road lead us to a short nature trail that Liz wanted to hike. At the trailhead, we found the path obscured by summer growth. We peered down the brushy trail just as a large water moccasin crawled out, dark with age. We froze. The snake slowly traversed the road just in front of us, seemingly unaware of our presence. In my mind, it seemed as large as a tyrannosaurus. "I'm not going in there," I told Liz, nodding toward the trail. "That makes six venomous snakes we've seen on this trip and not one nonvenomous snake."

"Okay, okay," she agreed.

"So why are we doing this trip in early September?"

Liz rolled her eyes.

We chose to hike the unpaved road instead of the overgrown path so we could more easily spot reptilian friends. It felt good to stretch our legs, though the temperature approached 100 degrees. "It's hotter than a two-peckered billy goat," exclaimed Liz, reflecting her farm upbringing. "Or a whorehouse on dollar day, or a . . ."

"All right, enough with the analogies."

We were starting to ration water; we had used more than expected since Keaton Beach, our last refill spot. There seemed no relief from the sun or heat. Sweat streamed down my face—precious water.

"I sure hope that fisherman is back when we return to the landing," said Liz, referring to a truck and boat trailer we had seen. "I'm getting parched. Maybe we can Yogi and Booboo some water." Yogi and Booboo, cartoon bears who frequently stole food in Jellystone Park, was Liz's term for getting something for free. "What do you think he has in that ice cooler in the back?" she asked.

"Cold drinks, I bet," I said wistfully, "and ice."

We walked a few more steps before Liz abruptly stopped. I froze, scanning the road for snakes. "I think I hear a boat," she said. "Let's head back."

We quickly walked the half mile to the landing, where we found a gray-haired fisherman loading his boat onto a trailer. We made a beeline and introduced ourselves. Herb Bennett showed off a nice mess of trout he had caught at the mouth of the creek. "I wasn't having any luck until I started back," he said, flashing a satisfied grin.

Herb said he lived near Lake Delancy in the Ocala National Forest. I had friends who lived along Lake Delancy, a Creek Indian family, and he knew them well. Florida now has more than 16 million people, but it always amazes me how connections can be made, especially in such a remote area. I knew then it was time to pop the question.

"Say Herb, do you have any extra water you could spare? We didn't pick up enough at the last stop." I felt like a panhandler. No matter how independent and well prepared you think you are, sometimes you have to ask for help. It's one of life's lessons.

Herb lifted a half-filled canteen. "You can have what I got left," he said. "Sorry I don't have any more." We poured his precious liquid into a water bottle, not spilling a drop. He must have noticed the desperate look in our eyes and the careful way we handled the water. "I do have some cold sodas!" he added. Herb smiled and opened his cooler, reaching in with a sunburned arm. Our eyes widened in anticipation as a puff of cold air rose up. He handed Liz a Bubba Cola, a brand we had never seen. He placed a cold root beer in my hand. I normally don't drink soda, but on this day it was a welcome treat. We thanked Herb profusely.

"Be sure to say hello to Becky and David for me," I said.

"Sure will," Herb promised. "Ya'll be careful now."

Acts of kindness, something as simple as a cold drink and friendly smile, always warm my heart.

Native people, too, had to replenish freshwater supplies while journeying along the coast. They likely knew the location of springs, or they paddled far enough up creeks and rivers to escape the influence of salt or brackish water.

We camped at the mouth of Dallus Creek in a tree-covered hammock surrounded by marsh. There was no evidence of humans other than a state survey marker. Animal signs included white feathers and feces left by egrets that had perched in the weathered live oaks. "It looks like the Australian bush or African savannahs," observed Liz, scanning the waist-high grass.

The place had a prehistoric feel. I could easily envision a time when sea levels were lower and the vast sea grass beds of the Big Bend coast were open prairies. I could almost see and hear a Paleo-Indian hunting camp: men laughing and joking, women cautioning children—words and signs of a forgotten language. All imagination? The effects of dehydration? Maybe, but that is what the spot evoked.

Twelve thousand years ago, during the Pleistocene epoch, the Big Bend Coast was a far different place than it is today. Mastodons, Columbian mammoths, giant sloths, huge armadillos and tortoises, bears, wolves, antelope, wild camels and horses, tapirs, capybaras, peccaries, and many other animals now extirpated from Florida once roamed arid prairies. Early hunters used a spear-throwing device known as an atlatl, a short wood shaft with an attached animal tooth or piece of bone, antler or stone where the bottom of a spear could be inserted. The atlatl gave early hunters more power to hurl spears at thick-hided animals, such as mastodon. The bow and arrow had not yet emerged on the scene.

The water table and sea level were much lower in the Pleistocene, and freshwater was mainly available along dry riverbeds in deep sinkholes. The major camps and kill sites of animals were along these sinks, many of which are today inundated by seawater. Archaeologists have followed former river channels several miles into the Gulf, especially the Aucilla, and have found numerous Paleo-Indian artifacts.

The climate for Florida's early Paleo-Indian people was probably cooler. Dust storms may have been commonplace since researchers found abundant quantities of dirt that had blown in from western parts of the continent. Theories abound as to why mastodons, mammoths, and other megafauna became extinct around ten thousand years ago. Did early native hunters wipe them out? Did climate change and rising sea level contribute to their demise? Did outbreaks of disease strike them down? We may never know.

My archaeologist friend Dan Penton has studied several archaeological sites along the Big Bend coast. He has helped to create pictures in my mind of how early people lived, especially those indigenous groups who ventured to the coast after the Pleistocene, when sea level and the water table were on the rise. "The reason for the coastal encampments was to take advantage of the stable food resources, especially on a seasonal basis," he told me. "Jack crevalle, mackerel, and a few other fish were seasonally specific. You could anticipate when they were going to be coming through. And especially with the jack crevalle, they were obviously filleting and smoking them. From archaeological records we know that's what they did.

"They were working around two parameters. For one, the insect problem was severe at certain times [something to which Liz and I could certainly relate]. The other is that it's a pretty raw place to be in the winter. So I think they were probably coming down in the late summer or fall to take advantage of the Jack crevalle run, and mullet. Also, the bay scallops were at the maximum maturity for harvest, and they [the native people] were smoking oysters to augment their protein source. When agriculture became a major activity, that would have left the early spring and late fall to come down to the coast."

According to Dan, most of the early people migrated back and forth to the coast by dugout and by foot from as far away as south central Georgia. "Major rivers like the Apalachicola, Ochlockonee, and Suwannee were surely used as travel routes," he said. "So most of the migration patterns that you can see from the artifact records tend to be north and south, not east and west."

A few years ago, I helped archaeologist Frank Keel with a site survey along St. Teresa Beach, just west of where the Ochlockonee River spills into the Gulf. St. Teresa does not have the vast stretches of marsh and tidal creeks commonly seen along the paddling trail, and neither does it boast clear turquoise waters, palm trees, and stretches of sugar-white sand and high dunes. St. Teresa is a unique landscape of narrow beach broken by tree roots and stumps, with an exposed hardpan of black earth. Much of the beach slices into an oak-topped ridge. Everything about the place speaks of erosion and change.

Walking the shore, moving in and out to avoid waves, Frank and I picked up flat pieces of black Indian pottery. We examined them, rubbed the wet, smooth sides between our fingers, and put them back. "It's everywhere," he said.

The pottery sherds were remnants of a two-thousand-year-old village site. The Gulf of Mexico had washed away about half of it; the other half was part of an old primary dune ridge covered with old-growth live oak trees. When we climbed the ridge's high point, a strong offshore breeze greeted us; surely a similar breeze had offered welcome relief to native people facing insect swarms. A freshwater creek was a short walk away.

We moved through dense undergrowth and began digging a grid of test holes. Using an auger, we bore down several times. Over half of the holes brought up pottery, fish bones, and oyster shells. "If we get this much from little auger holes," said my expert companion, "you can imagine what else is down there." Frank carefully bagged the artifacts and labeled them. They would be part of a report on the site, a requirement before the area was developed. Like most archaeological work, surveys are usually done just before bulldozer blades touch the earth.

Despite its wild, unswimmable appearance, the great maw of development was honing in on St. Teresa Beach, courtesy of the St. Joe Company, Florida's largest private landowner. In recent years, St. Joe changed its primary focus from growing pine trees to developing prime real estate. St. Teresa is just one of many coastal sites that the company targeted for large cluster developments, developments so large that St. Joe seeks to reroute parts of U.S. Highway 98 to make room for more houses and businesses along the beach. For nature lovers, it is a hard change to swallow.

Farther west, near Port St. Joe, Panama City, and Fort Walton, the proposed developments are larger and more elaborate. The company is pushing for an airport near Panama City that may eventually rival the size of Tampa International. Even the name for this section of Florida is being changed. Evidently, the "Panhandle" doesn't conjure up images that might lure future homeowners. The company's new moniker for the area: "Florida's Great Northwest."

It is difficult to visit a place slated for development. You want to shout warnings to every tree, animal, and blade of grass, but a feeling of futility envelops you. It is like trying to stop the sun from setting.

I took heart in believing that the village site, a piece of wild historic Florida about an acre in size, would likely remain undisturbed. For the rest of the area, however, I mourned that it would never be the same in my lifetime. And there was little I could do about it.

After dark, Liz and I were greeted by a vast panorama of stars unmarred by human lights. Liz showed me the upside-down rabbit in the moon from Oriental mythology. "Can you see it?" she kept saying. "Can you see it?" I had to tilt my head sideways before I could; then it seemed obvious.

My friend and neighbor Dr. Howie Baer, a physicist at Florida State, often regales other neighbors and me with his insights about the cosmos. He speaks in detail of the Big Bang, black holes, pulsars, and distant suns. Sounding a bit like Carl Sagan, he said, "There are billions of stars, hundreds of thousands of galaxies, and probably hundreds of thousands of planets that harbor life which is too far away for us to see." His words send my imagination soaring.

On a clear night, I also like to spot constellations from Creek Indian mythology. There are raccoons, woodpeckers, turtles, and serpents. I like to gaze at the Pleiades. Near this cluster of stars, the Creeks say there is a "blow hole" through which Creator breathed life, animating everything inside the cosmos. The Creeks believe that when people die, their souls first travel west and then north along the Milky Way. Eventually, the souls settle at their ancestors' campfire near the Pleiades. This is why the stars along the Milky Way are often called "campfires of the departed."

Gazing into the sky along the mouth of Dallus Creek, all seemed believable. We were alone but not alone. Countless eyes were watching.

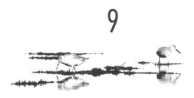

9

STEINHATCHEE

Stiff and sore, we arose on another clear day to the cries of wading birds and the whistle of an osprey. My mouth tasted salty; I was extremely thirsty. "We're probably a quart or two low [of water]," Liz estimated. We kicked ourselves for not picking up an extra gallon at Keaton Beach. I thought of the old adage "water, water everywhere . . ." We were wandering through a "desert" of salt water like generations of sailors before us, but we were merely uncomfortable, nothing like the desperate situation described in Coleridge's *The Rime of the Ancient Mariner*:

> Day after day, day after day,
> We stuck, nor breath nor motion;
> As idle as a painted ship
> Upon a painted ocean.
>
> Water, water every where
> And all the boards did shrink;
> Water, water every where,
> Nor any drop to drink.

We embarked at low tide, our thirst driving us, and waded and pulled the kayaks offshore a hundred yards or so. Once the water was about six inches deep, we could sit in our boats and push off the bottom. Ahead of us, a half mile offshore, egrets and herons stood like sentinels, fishing in inches-deep water. We had to move beyond them in order to paddle with ease.

The Big Bend is a low-relief coast, meaning that it slopes gradually. Motorboats, with the exception of airboats, do not venture close to shore ex-

Liz poses with Henry Garcia of Steinhatchee, owner of the West Wind Fish Camp.
Henry loaned us his old Ford pickup to drive around town.

cept near high tide. When low tide does trap a boat, the operators often try
to motor their way out, cutting long scars in the sea grass beds, a damaging
activity known as prop dredging. It's like racing a car across wet lawn grass.
We saw multiple examples of prop dredging as we approached Steinhatchee. The wounds take years to heal.

Our next landing spot was the Westwind Fish Camp, where Liz and I had
reserved motel rooms. After six days of paddling and eating freeze-dried
food, we were looking forward to a town break.

Owner Henry Garcia graciously greeted us and handed us two cold
bottles of freshwater. The water glittered in the sun like precious metal. Our
welcome angel extended other courtesies such as free use of his washer and
dryer and use of his old Ford pickup. The truck was one of those great faded
heaps in which you turn the ignition, flip a switch, and press a button to
start it up. A melon plant grew in a heap of dirt in the truck bed and snaked
its way toward the tailgate. A folded-up chair lay in the back, the kind used
to strap someone in a boat while he or she battled a large fish, such as a
tarpon. Liz called it a "fighting chair." Braking that old pickup required
good leg power, but we were grateful for the truck. We drove around feeling
like two hands just in from the farm.

We stopped for lunch at the Bridge End Café, just below the bridge over the Steinhatchee River. Old-timers are proud of the wide bridge. Many remember a ferry where cars and trucks often rolled into the water if not properly secured. Nowadays, local citizens frequently stop to make cell phone calls, the high bridge being one of the few places where there is good reception.

I had hoped that Steinhatchee would turn out to be a friendly trail town. So far, the signs looked promising.

Late in the day, back on Henry's dock, we watched a busy bird rookery across the inlet. A rookery is a noisy affair where every egret, heron, ibis, cormorant, and pelican seems to require its own zone of personal space. The egrets and herons, especially, defend their domains with raucous warnings and jabbing thrusts with long sharp beaks. A new bird flies in at great personal peril, especially when most available branches are occupied.

Leo Lovel, in his *Spring Creek Chronicles*, described what happened when a brown pelican stole a fish head from a great blue heron:

> the heron takes one step toward the pelican, silent as can be, and while the pelican is trying to swallow the fish head, the heron, with his six-inch long, inch and half wide, hard yellow beak, lays one mighty peck to the pelican's head.
>
> The pelican rises up straight, drops the mullet head from his mouth, and deflates like an old beach ball into a pile of brown feathers. Dead as a stone.

After dark, when the rookery calmed down, we walked to a nearby restaurant named Roy's and feasted on mullet and grouper. "One big feed will do me for a while," said Liz, "like a gator on a hog." On an earlier visit, we had dined at another fine restaurant called Fiddlers. We've always had good meals in Steinhatchee.

The next day, I awoke before dawn to the excited voices of recreational fishermen readying their gear, starting their boat motors, and purring their way to the Gulf. A great host of birds awakened, too, with raucous cries—egrets, herons, cormorants, and pelicans. They, too, were beginning a daylong search for fish.

I stepped outside my motel room and caught a whiff of exhaust fumes, the distinct smell of outboard motors. However unhealthy, it brought back pleasant memories of early mornings with my father, when he would awaken my brothers and me for predawn fishing trips. As we nibbled on toast or Pop Tarts in the car, our excitement grew. We'd launch in sync with the sunrise, and Dad would crank the smoky outboard; we'd wonder aloud about the luck that awaited us. Our most successful fishing adventure was offshore from Cedar Key, when we reeled in a seemingly unlimited supply of silver sea trout. We stopped at thirty.

My boyhood excitement was now magnified in Steinhatchee. Recreational fishing is big business, as evidenced by the line of marinas and motels along the lower river. It is a town that awakens early, especially when the fish are biting.

The morning scene would have been different a decade or more before. Instead of just recreational fishermen, or the multitudes of summer scallopers, mullet fishermen in their unique skiffs would have been heading out into the Gulf to net striped mullet with large gill nets, a kind of fishing that began with the first Native Americans and continued with the development of Florida's commercial fisheries in the late 1800s.

But several events led to a 1995 constitutional amendment that banned gill netting in Florida waters. For one, a growing demand for mullet eggs or roe in the Far East caused mullet fishing to intensify in the late 1970s. Egg-laying females were targeted, causing a decline in reproduction rates and overall numbers. Recreational fishermen worried that a mullet collapse would reverberate through the food chain, resulting in less food for popular game fish such as snook, redfish, trout, and tarpon. Others voiced concerns about the effects of netting on sea turtles, manatees, porpoises, and birds.

Commercial fishing interests blocked or delayed most proposed regulations on their industry by flooding hearings with net fishermen and by filing court motions. Recreational fishermen, inspired by bans enacted by California and Texas, responded with a net ban proposal. Their champion was Karl Wickstrom, former investigative reporter with the *Miami Herald* and publisher of *Florida Sportsman* magazine. Wickstrom pushed for a Florida ban in his magazine and through the Florida Conservation Association. Proponents needed more than 400,000 signatures to place it on the 1994 ballot. They garnered 201,649 in one day by working polling places during the 1992 election, possibly the most successful one-day petition effort in America up to that time. Strong endorsements from public figures such as General "Stormin' Norman" Schwarzkopf furthered their cause.

Wickstrom portrayed commercial fishermen as villains. "The sport fishing people, you get down to a few fish, they'll figure out how to save them," he said. "The commercial people, they'll figure out who gets them."

Opponents of the ban began to see themselves as David versus Goliath. They were losing the public relations campaign both in terms of money and exposure. Their arguments that the mullet fishery had not collapsed and that their trade was far less harmful to birds, turtles, and other protected species than sport fishing's barbed hooks and monofilament line failed to reach the broader public. They complained that large contributions from developers and sport-fishing equipment manufacturers were largely funding the net ban movement. "Just like what was done with the Indians, they're trying to get the commercial fishermen out of the way so they can develop the coast," argued Jack Rudloe, a Panacea activist who often spoke on behalf of the mullet fishermen.

The net ban passed overwhelmingly, garnering 72 percent of the vote. Robert P. Jones, executive director of the Southeastern Fisheries Association, tried to frame the outcome from a historical perspective: "The hunter-gatherer culture of the commercial fishermen was bound to run head-on into a new culture in Florida brought about through the influx of new families to the state at an alarming pace after the end of World War II," he wrote. "Many cultures have been forced to change because of war or through the ever expanding need for more turf."

While recreational fishermen touted a quick recovery of certain fish populations, many Big Bend coastal fishermen were devastated. Most were third- and fourth-generation mullet netters. Some graduated to inland jobs or shifted to commercial crabbing and aquaculture; others struggled to net mullet with legal cast nets or attempted to flout or challenge the law. Leo Lovel, in *Spring Creek Chronicles*, writes about using a net he had used for decades, one now illegal:

> For some reason on this day, I just don't give a damn. I don't care if the helicopter comes, the plane starts dive-bombing or the whole Marine Patrol roars in on me. I'm gonna enjoy this. I'm gonna enjoy picking every fish, digging every oyster burr out, bolting every inch of this now illegal net on the boat. Taking my time, thanking the Great Maker for every fish, every minute I've gotten to spend on His bountiful sea.

I witnessed the changes brought about by the net ban in Lovel's small Big Bend fishing village, Spring Creek. Spring Creek once bustled with activity

Even after dark, Spears Seafood along Spring Creek was a thriving business. The building was situated on the largest of the burgeoning freshwater springs that gave the place its name.

Here's a photo I took in 1977 of Spring Creek, then a busy fishing village along the Big Bend coast between Panacea and St. Marks.

The Spring Creek of today has a ghostly feel. Many residents blame the 1995 passage of the net ban that inhibited commercial fishermen from catching mullet and other fish.

around seafood outlets and net-draped piers. Nearly everything spoke or smelled of mullet.

Mullet skiffs would come and go and anchor near the largest of the burgeoning freshwater springs that gave the place its name. On any given day, workers and fishermen unloaded, weighed, sorted, and cleaned mullet and other fish, some freshly caught in the visible labyrinth of tidal creeks and marsh, others brought in from as far away as Pensacola and Cedar Key.

The spoils from all this activity—fish heads, guts, and fins—were always of great interest to an eclectic array of cats, dogs, brown pelicans, tri-colored herons, great egrets, and gulls. For as long as man has fished, this symbiosis with other creatures has existed.

"There's people who come down here and offer us money you wouldn't believe for this place," John Taylor told me, then manager of Spears Seafood. "They want to clear everything and build condominiums. But we want to keep this place just like it is."

At day's end, fishing families congregated on the docks and in the seafood houses. One could hear talk of the latest catches and prices along with local gossip. In the background, a marshy expanse turned crimson, the last boats pulled in, and birds returned to the wild. All the while, the clear freshwater spring pumped out untold gallons a minute, a never-ending flow, it seemed.

The Spring Creek of today has a ghostly feel. The old café near the docks is in ruins, its neon sign intact but tilted. Spears Seafood, perched on the largest spring, stands empty. A tall wooden fence, liberally plastered with "No Trespassing" signs, bars access to the spring.

A sign, standing inside a beached mullet skiff in front of the still-open Spring Creek Restaurant, explains what happened: "This was one of the famous 'net boats' or 'mullet skiffs' that was outlawed by Article X of the Florida Constitution in 1995. This type of boat and gear, fished by a commercial fisherman, was the most productive and selective fishing machine ever invented. It was also involved in the most regulated fishery in the history of the world. The Article X amendment not only outlawed these nets and this design of boat, it ended a culture, an economy and independent American way of life that had been a major part of this state since the beginning of its history."

For me, the bitter sign instilled a pang of guilt. I had voted for Article X, the net ban. I had grown weary of the stalemate over regulations while fish populations suffered. Now, more than a decade later, I yearn for middle ground. Can we conserve fish populations and still preserve a culture? Perhaps a new article of the Florida Constitution can be drafted and put forth to voters, one grudgingly supported by a majority of those involved. Commercial and recreational fishermen can share the same waters, divide the catch, and still leave enough to perpetuate the species. And the fish houses of Spring Creek will once again bustle with activity.

10

LIVING HISTORY

Fully hydrated and rested, we paddled out of Steinhatchee, steering just clear of the busy boat channel. The river was coffee-colored from tannic acids produced by leaves, bark, and aquatic vegetation. It darkened the Gulf for two or three miles before we could again gaze wondrously into the water. We began seeing more rays, and big ones; they often left a wake when surprised. The bottom was rockier in places, too.

We paddled across a glassy, mirrorlike surface. Offshore boats seemed to float in air, like ghostly mirages in a field of blue. It was the calmest day yet, although Hurricane Isabel churned in the tropics, days away from possible landfall.

I was enjoying the now-familiar natural high derived from steady physical activity in a beautiful setting. My confidence in my physical abilities was high. I no longer worried whether my middle-aged body could handle the rigors of the trip. My arms and shoulders felt hulklike while my spirit seemed infused with childlike innocence. There was time to notice cloud shapes and every subtle change in wind. I often found myself softly singing and thinking fond thoughts of friends and family. I was reminded of an English man whom I had met years before. I asked him if he believed in God or a supreme being. I loved his reply. "I'm not sure," he replied in a sophisticated accent, "but I do find myself having godly thoughts now and then." Perhaps every journey is a search for meaning in life.

The rising tide easily floated us up Sink Creek to a small brackish spring. Adjacent to the deep limestone crevice was a remote landing and a grove of live oak and slash pine. We admired low, fernlike coontie palms with their pineapplelike cones, an ancient native of Florida. The rootlike stem of coontie palm was a main source of starch for native people and early settlers; it was once harvested to near depletion. I often wonder how early native people figured out how to remove the poisonous alkaloids from the crushed pulp by washing, fermenting, and then washing again. Trial and error? Inadequately prepared coontie roots were blamed in the death of one of Hernando de Soto's men and in the deaths of several Union soldiers in Florida. Perhaps unwelcome visitors were not given proper instructions about preparing native cuisine.

Coontie was a main staple of Seminole Indians on the run because it could be quickly harvested in the wild, reducing the need for cultivated gardens. Could Seminoles have utilized this spot at Sink Creek? I wondered. There are no records, but numerous accounts describe the headwaters area as an active fishing and trading spot in the early 1900s. Arriving by mule- or oxen-drawn wagons, local families camped on one side of the hammock, while farmers from neighboring counties camped on the other.

The farmers came to trade sweet potatoes, corn, syrup, and other goods for fish. They would stay until enough fish had been caught and salted. A "seep well" provided freshwater for people and animals, and a fish house was built.

Evonne Cline, whose roots reach back to the first white settlers of the area, has chronicled most of Sink Creek's history. I caught up with her when Liz and I did a presentation on the paddling trail for the Dixie County Historical Society in Old Town. "My father and grandfather fished out there at Sink Creek," she said. "They told me how they lived. The fish house backed up to those boils. The islands on each side of the creek were named after people who camped there. They went there in the fall when the crops were in and the mullet roe was big."

You can't do historical research in Dixie County without coming across Evonne's name. She's been recording oral history and family genealogy since the mid-1960s. "When I got started, I was just researching my family's history," she said. "Then it mushroomed. Other families wanted information and I couldn't tell them no because I loved doing it. I'm so glad I got the ones I have [interviews] because many have passed on. There's more people I want to talk to, but I'm getting tired."

Part of her research involves combing the woods for nearly forgotten cemeteries. "We've got many turpentine camp sites in this county," she said, "and there were lots of deaths in those camps. There were cemeteries for those that died, but most have no stones. Mostly blacks worked in those camps.

"There was a turpentine camp near Sink Creek. One big oak tree stands where it was. No pine trees were planted there."

Turpentining—the process of harvesting and distilling the crude gum of longleaf and slash pines—thrived in Florida from the 1880s to the 1940s. The industry not only depended upon a large supply of mature pines, it also developed a system of labor exploitation that bordered on slavery. Black men were often shanghaied to work in remote turpentine camps, far from their homes.

Camp commissaries were set up according to the classic migrant worker Catch-22. Goods were sold at highly inflated prices and a tab was kept for every worker. At the end of the season, a worker was lucky to break even. Two verses from an old turpentine song describe the arrangement:

> They worked this nigger all year long;
> It's time for him to go home.
> You hear the Bossman say to the Bookkeeper,
> "How do this nigger stand?"

> The Bookkeeper goes in the office,
> He sit down and 'gin to figger;
> Then he say to the Bossman,
> "That nigger's just even now!"

Workers generally earned from $1.00 to $1.75 a day (in the late 1930s), depending on the number of trees chipped, cups dipped, and barrels filled. Poor weather or dips in the market could affect workers' income for long stretches of time. One white manager of eight turpentine camps near Opal, Florida, in 1922 described what happened during a lengthy rainy period: "It poured down bullfrogs for weeks, and water stood knee-deep all over the woods. We had to set in camp and do nothing. Besides the four hundred niggers, there was thirty head of horses and mules eatin' up rations; and the wet weather made the horses' and mules' backs so sore we couldn't have worked even if it had stopped rainin'. I shore had a peck of trouble on my hands. To make everything worse, the big bosses in New York kept tele-graphin' me wantin' to know why no production. Finally I got mad, told 'em to go to hell, and waded off the job."

I live in a remnant longleaf forest near Woodville, south of Tallahassee. After a prescribed burn on my property, scattered sherds of red-brick turpentine cups lay exposed on the blackened earth, and I wonder about the souls who once worked the trees. It is difficult to contrast the lives of turpentiners with the peace of the piney woods. Likewise, it is hard to picture human toil and suffering when paddling along blankets of marsh grass or shoreline walls of second-growth forest.

In the late 1930s, as part of the Florida Writers' Project of the Works Progress Administration, Stetson Kennedy, Robert Cook, and Zora Neale Hurston ventured into a Cross City turpentine camp in Dixie County. Kennedy later described the visit:

> we had gained access by telling the (heavily armed) owners we were looking for songs. We set up a night-time recording session around a campfire. In between songs, I said to the "hands," "Don't you know they can't make you work against your will?"
>
> "They do do it," was the answer.
>
> "Then why don't you leave and get out of it?"
>
> "The onliest way out is to die out. If you tries to leave, they will kill you, and you will have to die, because they got peoples to bury you out in them woods."
>
> At this point several young men jumped up and disappeared into the underbrush—to serve as sentries in case one of the white woodsriders were to show up.
>
> Sure enough, after a while one of the sentries rushed into the firelight urgently whispering, "Here come the Man! Sing somethin', quick!"

Race relations were equally tumultuous in neighboring counties. J. C. Powell, who captained a Florida convict camp in the late 1800s, wrote this chilling account:

> I do not suppose that there are over a half a dozen colored families in Taylor County, and when a Negro passes through he goes on a run. To illustrate; the natives had formerly a favorite amusement which consisted of organizing a bear-hunt and inviting one darky to accompany the party. He would invariably be missing when they returned, and they would report sorrowfully that he had gone into a swamp after a bear and that the beast had eaten him. Finally the appetite of Taylor

County bears for Negroes became so notorious that no black man would consent to join in sport of that character.

The 1910s and 1920s marked major setbacks in race relations in many parts of the country. The Ku Klux Klan ran amok, often in cahoots with law enforcement and government officials; it seemed to be open season on African-Americans. Though outnumbered and outgunned, some blacks armed themselves and fought back, perhaps drawing strength from the brave words of Claude McKay in his 1919 poem "If We Must Die."

If we must die, let it not be like hogs
Hunted and penned in an inglorious spot,
While round us bark the mad and hungry dogs,
Making their mock at our accursed lot.

If we must die, O let us nobly die,
So that our precious blood may not be shed
In vain; then even the monsters we defy
Shall be constrained to honor us though dead!

O kinsmen! We must meet the common foe!
Though far outnumbered let us show us brave,
And for their thousand blows deal one deathblow!
What though before us lies the open grave?

Like men we'll face the murderous, cowardly pack,
Pressed to the wall, dying, but fighting back!

The infamous Rosewood massacre of 1923 occurred in Levy County near Cedar Key. The trouble began when a white woman accused a black man of assault. A mob descended upon the town looking for the alleged perpetrator. Two white men were shot as they stormed a house, but in the end, the entire town was torched and several residents were killed. The twenty black families of Rosewood fled to Gainesville, never to return.

Less than a month before the Rosewood massacre, a black man had been accused of murdering a white schoolteacher in Perry. He was burned at the stake, and a black church, Masonic lodge, and meeting hall were also torched. Can time possibly heal such savage wounds? In today's more open society, perhaps the echoes of past atrocities are fading.

Evonne Cline claims that race relations are improving in Dixie County. "Most everybody, whites and blacks, have worked real hard just to get by here. There's not a lot of difference in salaries or in the way people live. Everybody works together, and they're real protective of each other. Most of the trouble's been from people who aren't from around here."

Pointing to a different example of the early days, Evonne showed me her research about the Putnam Lumber Company in Dixie County, which operated from the 1920s until the mid-1940s. The company set up complete, segregated neighborhoods for the white and black workers, including commissaries, bars, and churches. The black neighborhood was called "Black Bottom." Workers were paid equal salaries—ten cents an hour in the 1920s, rising to twenty-four cents an hour a few years later. White and black workers often worked side by side.

Evonne interviewed her father, Lester Valentine, about cutting dead heart pine, or "lighter wood," for the lumber trains: "If you've never used a 'gatortail' cross-cut saw, you've really missed some hard work," he said. "We sawed till our arms felt like they was going to fall off. Our day started at daylight and ended at dark."

When the lumber company folded, everyone felt the pinch, and black workers faced a new dilemma. The company sold the cemetery they had provided for them, known as "ghost's bar," and since segregation was still enforced, even for dead people, blacks were suddenly left with no place to bury their dead. Church elders agonized over the problem.

In *Cemeteries of Dixie County*, published by the historical society, Princess Lucille G. Stockton writes: "As Elder Glanton searched and inquired, God placed in his heart to talk to Mr. and Mrs. J. Clayton Welch [a white couple]. After explaining the situation, he asked if they would sell the Black people a piece of property for a cemetery. Mr. Welch said to him: 'No, we will not sell you the land, we will gladly donate property for this purpose.' Thus the site was chosen, agreed upon and given by the grantees, the now Dixie County Memorial Cemetery."

Evonne feels strongly about preserving the history of Dixie County for all of its residents and their descendants. "Memories are fading," she laments, "soon to be no more." She sighs when discussing recent changes. "I never thought I'd see condominiums in Horseshoe Beach, but there's two of them coming, and every unit is already sold—and they're not even built yet.

"I can't tell you what my aunt said about it [the development], but they're bringing in new water and sewer systems, and paved roads. Course, our taxes are all going up. Most of the older people in the small fishing communities are selling their places and moving farther out into the country, away from the coast, where they can afford to live. That's called progress and development, I guess."

She paused, seeming to search for a positive spin. "I guess I can't be selfish 'cause the coast is such a beautiful place, as long as they [newcomers] benefit the county in some way. I love the sunsets, love the woods. I can see why people want out of Miami and those other big cities, where all you see is concrete and cars."

Evonne is also seeing a rising tide of ecotourists. "Have you been to the Road to Nowhere?" she asked. I nodded. County Road 361 near Jena is a straight, wide road through salt marsh built by corrupt county officials in the 1970s so drug smuggling planes could land. The road abruptly ends at no particular destination, no town or dwellings or boat landing, simply marsh. "A lot of birdwatchers like going to the Road to Nowhere. It's really pretty along there, so it's turned into something positive."

Exploring Sink Creek, relishing the shade of massive live oaks and dodging small sinkholes ringed by feisty blue crabs, I tried to picture the early times—rowboats heading down the creek to net mullet, busy hands cleaning and salting the catch, flickering campfires illuminating weathered faces and animated storytelling. I gave silent thanks for people like Evonne Cline who dutifully record the memories.

At our lovely streamside camp beside Sink Creek, Liz and I took an evening stroll along the salt flats, a sinuous border of sand between the marsh and islandlike tree hammocks. This relatively high ground, flushed by tides only a few times a month, is so concentrated with crystallized salt from evaporation that nearly all plant life is suppressed. It makes for easy walking, except for the armies of small marching fiddler crabs. The sand and grass was alive with them, each male bearing an oversized pincher. We had to be careful not to step on any. I had heard that some marshes could contain 150,000 fiddler crabs per acre; the figure was totally believable.

None of the crabs stayed still long enough for us to glimpse their fiddling motion. When the male repeatedly picks up food from the ground and brings it to its mouth, partially obscured by the big claw, it can resemble

From our Sink Creek camp, we strolled through a graveyard of dead cedars, a natural sculpture garden that was further evidence of rising sea levels. Here Liz stands on a dead cedar and looks out over a remote wilderness of marsh and hammocks.

someone moving a bow across a fiddle, thus the name fiddler crab. Weighing as much as half of the crab, the big claw is used for fighting, bluffing, and attracting females.

Perhaps as a way of identifying themselves in the roving herd, fiddler males court by rhythmically waving their big claws and raising them higher and higher until almost tipping over. If a female shows interest, he will rush back and forth to the entrance of his burrow as if to show her the way. He'll crawl inside and beat on the walls with his big claw until the female enters. Then he'll guide her to a mating chamber.

We strolled through a graveyard of dead cedars, a natural sculpture garden that was further evidence of rising sea levels. Looking out over marshy expanses, we were reminded once again that this was the most remote stretch of land along the Gulf coast. I wasn't growing tired of it. No signs of humans could be seen, and we could see for miles. It was, simply, pristine country. If Florida's largest chunk of wilderness is the Everglades, then this was Florida's longest coastal wilderness.

Although I knew more intensive development was coming to the Big Bend coast, I felt comforted in knowing that more than three-quarters of it is in public ownership. With proper stewardship, it will remain for generations to enjoy, a type of living history.

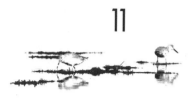

11

TURTLES AND PIRATES

Before breakfast, we paddled again to the Sink Creek headwaters, this time at low tide. The spring boil was clearly visible. The water was tea-colored and brackish, but perfect for a refreshing dip.

Gliding into the clear waters of the Gulf again, we scared up small rays. Blue crabs crouched boldly in sea grass, pinchers ready, before quickly retreating. The crabs also performed a curious activity. They would swim to the surface and churn the water like little eggbeaters, perhaps to obtain more oxygen.

An occasional redfish hunted in the shallow grass, dorsal fins exposed. Smaller fish darted in various directions, and leaping and splashing striped mullet added an exclamation point to the abundance.

I like to think mullet jump out of sheer joy, but scientists have put forth several theories: they leap to dislodge parasites, to flee predators, to disgorge sand (since they often graze along the bottom), to impress the opposite sex (by distinguishing themselves from the pack—"look at me, I can really jump!"), and, my favorite, to pass gas. In other words, some theorize that mullet cannot fart underwater.

One of few thorough studies on the subject found that mullet jump more frequently during warm weather. Researchers noted that fishes living in hot, low-oxygen waters have developed mechanisms for breathing oxygen not only through the water but also through the air. Mullet, they theorize, being an active schooling fish, need more oxygen so they jump to gulp air. Whatever the reason, it is a curious, age-old phenomenon that spiced up our trip.

Once we were in deeper water, sea turtles popped up heads before dashing underwater, an everyday occurrence. Most likely they were green, loggerhead, or Kemp's ridley sea turtles. Many were on incredible migratory journeys that would take them thousands of miles, navigating by detecting subtle differences in the earth's magnetic field. Sea turtles along the Big Bend coast have not been extensively studied, mainly because the expansive stretches of salt marsh are not suitable sea turtle nesting habitat. A map of loggerhead nesting activities, for example—90 percent of which occurs in Florida—shows nesting in every coastal county except for those along the Big Bend coast. A startling 62,905 loggerhead nests were recorded on Florida beaches in 2002.

All five species of Florida sea turtles are endangered; the Kemp's ridley is the most endangered in the world, with adult numbers estimated at five thousand. Overharvesting of turtle eggs, destruction of beach nesting areas, and turtles being hooked or caught in nets are major causes of the decline. Turtles have also been killed for meat, shells, leather, perfumes, and cosmetics, practices that continue in other countries.

Florida's coastal pioneers depended heavily on sea turtles for meat. A graphic account of butchering and cooking turtle meat is contained in a memoir of Mrs. Isabelle (Johansen) Hanlon, published in a 1960 newspaper column by historian Josephine Cortes:

> Many nights papa would be either too tired to sleep, or it would be too hot. On those occasions he would walk up and down the beach within a mile and half of our house and turn from one to three turtles a night.
>
> He would turn them on their backs and learned just exactly how to stick them to kill them quickly. He left them there until the next morning when they would be butchered.
>
> Papa made a yoke to carry the meat home in buckets across his shoulders. He would be up very early in the morning in order to get the butchering done and the meat brought in before he rowed across the bay to work at the sawmill. My sister Ruth and I always had to go with him to help carry the meat home.
>
> The meat was cut in sections to make a large roast. Then he would leave the whole thing for mother and us girls to clean. All fat and leaders, which were plentiful, had to be trimmed off. Papa built a nice big table and benches under a large oak tree, and there we sat, sometimes all day, cleaning the meat. Mother knew just how to cure it. She rubbed

it with very coarse salt, then laid the meat on long boards to drain the blood. This would sometimes take a couple of days. Then she packed it down in layers in large wooden candy tubs that we got at the store on the mainland. Finally she cooked up a salt brine and covered the meat completely.

Every so often she would have to reheat the brine. The meat kept perfectly. We would sometimes have a tub left until the next turtle season. The largest turtle that father ever turned produced seventy-five pounds of meat after it was cleaned, ready to salt.

When mother wanted to serve turtle meat, she would put it in a large pan of water the night before and change the water several times to rinse all the brine off the meat. She roasted it with bay leaves and whole allspice. The result was a very tender, tasty meal—with mother's wonderful brown gravy.

Mrs. Hanlon went on the say that they pickled the flippers like pig's feet, and her father used the turtle fat to grease machinery in the sawmill. Very little was wasted. "It was not so much a question of saving money as it was of learning to do for yourself," she concluded. "To live off the land and sea in order to survive."

The export trade was a different story. Thousands of the huge reptiles were captured off the Gulf coast and penned in Cedar Key before being shipped to outside markets. Before butchering, the turtles were often kept alive by turning them on their backs and keeping them in shaded areas. Green turtles were especially prized, partly for their calipee, the fat attached to the lower shell that became stock for the popular green turtle soup.

Florida's famous naturalist, the late Archie Carr, in his classic *The Sea Turtle: So Excellent a Fishe*, expounded on the green turtle's edibility from a historical perspective:

A green turtle was as big as a heifer, easy to catch, and easy to keep alive on its back in a space no greater than itself. It was an ideal food resource, and it went into the cooking pots of the salt-water peasantry and tureens of the flagships alike. It fed a host of people and to some of them it became a dish of almost ceremonial stature. In England the green turtle came to be known as the London Alderman's Turtle, because an Alderman's Banquet was considered grossly incomplete if it failed to begin with clear green turtle soup.

By 1878, fifteen thousand green turtles a year were being shipped from Florida and the Caribbean to England. It was the Great Plains buffalo slaughter in a marine environment, and the outcome was just as predictable. By the early 1900s, large sea turtles were becoming scarce, and the market collapsed.

The Kemp's ridley has been slowly rebounding after a massive conservation effort. The Big Bend coast is one of its main haunts, although its primary nesting beaches were long a mystery to scientists. Finally, in the 1960s, Dr. Henry Hildebrand found a 1947 film by a Mexican engineer that showed an estimated forty thousand Kemp's ridleys nesting along the Mexican Gulf coast at Rancho Nuevo in broad daylight as part of an *arribada*, Spanish for "arrival." Archie Carr described his reaction to seeing the film after a long and futile search for Kemp's ridley nests:

> the world suddenly seemed to me a place in which anything can happen.
>
> The film was short. It was shaky in places, faded with time, and rainy with scratches. But it was the cinema of the year all the same, the picture of the decade. For me really, it was the movie of all time. For me, personally, as a searcher after ridleys for twenty years, as the chronicler of the oddness of ridleys, the film outdid everything from *Birth of a Nation* to *Zorba the Greek*.

Sadly, due to egg harvesting and other activities, Carr and others found that the number of Kemp's ridley nests along Rancho Nuevo had dropped to only a few hundred since the 1940s.

Kemp's ridleys have been showing up along Florida beaches in recent years. In 2002, two nested in Pinellas County near Clearwater, and one nested on Florida's east coast.

Jack and Anne Rudloe of Panacea have worked tirelessly on behalf of the Kemp's ridley and other sea turtles through their marine lab and aquarium, Gulf Specimen. They often try to rehabilitate ridley turtles that have swallowed fishhooks.

On one occasion, when I brought a group of young people to the lab, Jack invited us to join him in releasing a rehabilitated ridley back into Dickerson Bay. The turtle had swallowed a hook and had been kept in a large aquarium for about a month. Life-threatening surgery was avoided when X-rays and metal detectors confirmed that the hook had passed

Author and activist Jack Rudloe of Panacea and his wife, Anne, have worked tirelessly on behalf of the Kemp's ridley and other sea turtles through their marine lab and aquarium, Gulf Specimen. They often try to rehabilitate ridley turtles that have swallowed fish hooks.

through the turtle's system. We carried the two-foot-long turtle to the bay, and Jack allowed two students to place it in the shallow water. The ridley quickly lunged toward deep water with its paddlelike flippers, swimming to freedom. It never looked back.

Jack and Anne envision a day when ridleys will again nest on Gulf coast beaches in mass numbers. On assignment for *National Geographic*, they traveled to Costa Rica to witness an *arribada* of olive ridley sea turtles, a close relative of the Kemp's ridley. Here's how Jack described it in *Florida Wildlife* magazine:

> Turtles plowed the black sands with their noses, turtles laid eggs, turtles went back to the sea. Wet turtles were in the surf, and dry turtles up on the beach; turtles crouched down in pits, digging nest chambers, while others kicked dirt into them, covering them up. . . . A mother turtle scooped out the white, half-developed eggs of an earlier nest, sending them rolling down the beach like ping-pong balls. The night was filled with "thump thump thump" as turtles heaved and wheezed, rocked back and forth, slammed plastrons down and packed the sand over finished eggs. . . . With a hundred thousand turtles in less than a mile of

beach, there was no room to sit or stand. Sand thrown by flippers of a turtle showered our legs. Tiny black hatchlings crawled into our laps as we scribbled notes.

I rounded a peninsula and spotted Liz crouched in a salt marsh. "If you're an American going into the marsh and you're an American coming out," she called out, "then what are you when you are in the marsh?"

"I have no idea."

"Eura-pee-in."

Besides essential bathroom stops for sea kayakers, salt marshes are nursery grounds for a multitude of life, a foundation for the coastal food chain. Hiding within the protective grasses are small fish, shrimp, shellfish, worms, snails, and crabs. Species of killifish spend their entire lives in marshes. Marsh grasses are continually being broken down by bacteria and fungi to form detritus, a vital food source for snails, worms, crustaceans, and fish.

Because the Big Bend is shallow, with mild wave action under normal conditions, sediments carried by rivers and streams easily settle to create a suitable environment for salt marshes to develop. And unlike the high-energy east coast, where marshes are normally found in protected bays and estuaries, the Big Bend's marshes lie along the open Gulf for long unbroken stretches. Two main types of grasses thrive in this environment—cordgrass and needlerush. Cordgrass is often closest to the water, while black needlerush grows in higher areas of the marsh. Throughout the trip, we had to be extremely careful when walking or paddling through the stiff needlerush or heeding a call of nature; the tips are extremely sharp.

Salt marshes, shallow water, and the lack of white sand beaches are reasons why the Big Bend coast has largely escaped intensive human development, a situation that is rapidly changing because land along popular beach areas is cost prohibitive or unavailable.

We paddled into a headwind and rested at a spot called Bowlegs Point. "I feel like we've gone ten miles already," said Liz, puffing. We had only paddled three.

Liz stressed that we must try to describe every potential hardship in the paddling guide. "Someone who is unprepared could get themselves killed," she said.

As if to emphasize the point, Liz bent over to retrieve a fishing bobber and was poked in the eye by a long strand of sharp needlerush. After a while, she said: "My eye is getting kind of gooey, like it has Vaseline in it. I guess that's part of the healing process." She yearned for antibiotic eye drops, but a doctor or pharmacy was two or more days away. Liz tied a bandanna over her damaged eye. With her dirty white shirt, flowery sarong, and neoprene booties, she looked like some kind of bizarre pirate.

After several days of paddling, our real names had transformed into nautical names. My new name was Captain Skanky, while Liz's was First Mate Scurvy. We often joked about being pirates, using the classic "hrrrr."

But pirating, in one form or another, has long been popular along remote inlets and bays of the Big Bend coast. Numerous tales of buried pirate treasure, such as along Deadman's Bay at the mouth of the Steinhatchee River, still intrigue visitors and residents. Like those Caribbean buccaneers, early Big Bend pirates generally consisted of French sailors, runaway slaves, deserters, and groups of people who had been persecuted by the Spanish. They shared a mutual hatred of the Spanish. After the American Revolution, many combined a fervent sense of red, white, and blue patriotism with an unquenchable lust for profit.

A specific account of Big Bend pirates involved the family of Don Tomas Mendez Marquez in 1682. Marquez owned a large spread near the Suwannee River known as Hacienda La Chua (Alachua). News of his wealth doubtlessly spread because a group of thirty-five French pirates, otherwise known as buccaneers, sailed up the river and captured Marquez and his family. They demanded ransom money and 150 head of cattle, but a band of Timucuan Indians rescued the family before the ransom was paid.

Preston Chavous, a Dixie County native who lives along the lower Suwannee River, is a local authority on area history. He recalled several stories of Big Bend pirates and their treasure. "Jean Lafitte brought stuff up the Suwannee River to Fowler's Bluff," he said. "In 1892, a fellow named Baird [Eberle Baird] showed up with a map and he come to Fowler's Bluff. They got the gold at Fowler's Bluff and took it to Gainesville in two wagons. They took it to the Dutton Bank and put it in the Dutton Bank [one of the earliest private banks in the state, founded around 1885]. Baird became a wealthy man, and he ended up owning a company called Baird Hardware. It was the big hardware company for this area.

"The pirates came up the Steinhatchee River, too. There's a lot of caves up the Steinhatchee River. Old man Howard is supposed to have found a lot of money up there at Jonesboro."

More contemporary pirate stories revolve around the Prohibition era, when gangster Al Capone's network allegedly used Big Bend rivers as ports of entry for bootleg liquor. "Uncle Harry said they would take it off a big ship and old man Oldund would flag them into here," said Preston Chavous. "The Suwannee was a big smuggling place because they had the railroad at Old Town. They'd bring it in here and take some and put it on a little boat and send it up the river to the railroad. If it didn't get caught, they'd send the big one up. Then they'd pack it in boxcars full of moss. It went to Al Capone in Chicago. That's very true. My uncle went to the federal penitentiary along with half of Gilchrist County in the '27 to '29 period. I've got my uncle's entire court case. They tried him in Pensacola. My other uncle got disbarred from practicing law for a year for trying to lie for him [his brother]."

Pirating continued in the late 1970s and early 1980s when drug runners utilized the Big Bend coast to take the heat off operations in south Florida. They found fertile ground due to the area's remoteness and the overall poverty of residents. In addition, the precedent for smuggling had already been set during Prohibition. "Some of the same families was involved," noted Preston Chavous.

"You gotta understand," one Dixie County resident explained to me. "You come to a man making a few hundred dollars a month and with a family, and offer him several thousand dollars for a night's work; that was tempting."

Eventually, a fee scale for a smuggling run was established: $10,000 for each bale handler; $20,000 for the deputy sheriffs, county officials, and truckers; $50,000 for offload crew organizers and other middlemen; and up to half a million dollars for executive managers. Commercial fishing for some people quickly turned into an occasional hobby.

But easy money doesn't always equate with wise decisions. "It was quick money, and most of them spent it immediately," observed Preston Chavous. "They just let it flow like water. They lived like kings; they'd never been able to have anything but an outhouse and a pitcher pump before."

The spending habits aroused the suspicions of federal agents and the Internal Revenue Service. One smuggler even installed a new swimming pool at his Steinhatchee residence so that offload crews could wash marijuana residue off their bodies before they went home. Government sting operations eventually unraveled the smuggling network. Stories of the era still abound.

"I was in the music store near Fanning Springs," began one man, "and there was this big guy in there wearing overalls. A man wearing a suit and tie walks in and the big guy suddenly decks him, knocking him back several feet. 'We don't want no damn narks around here!' he shouted at him.

"'But I'm a salesman from Tallahassee,' said the man on the ground.

"The big guy helped him up and brushed him off, apologizing the whole time."

I heard of one woman who was paid five thousand dollars to simply wait all night by a telephone booth and discreetly make a call to drug runners if law enforcement officials turned down a certain road. She never had to call, but she was paid the money.

Preston Chavous, who owned a title company, woke up one morning to find "more subpoenas than I could handle in my hands."

"I got all of my papers together and I went to the federal courthouse in downtown Jacksonville," he said. "They went to question me, and I answered every question. They wanted to see my books, and I showed them my books. They finally asked me, 'Mister Chavous, why did you take cash money?'

"I said, 'I was in business to make money.'

"'Did you know this was illegal money?'

"I said, 'No sir, because green money don't talk. I was desperate for money, and I needed it bad. I paid the income tax on it and I put it in the bank, and here's my deposit book if you want to see it.' They thought they had me, but they didn't have me because I didn't know nothing about the export-import business. I never was in the drug business."

Marine scientist Jack Rudloe wrote his first novel about Big Bend drug running. In the late 1970s, I ventured to his home on the shores of Dickerson Bay. I had enjoyed his books about Gulf Coast marine life and the adventures of being a marine specimen collector, so I curiously glanced at a dog-eared unfinished manuscript on his desk titled *Shrimper's Log*.

Shrimper's Log chronicled a year in the life of a Gulf Coast shrimper, but Rudloe was struggling with it, he told me. Drug smuggling had become rampant along the coast, and he was unsure how to realistically describe the temptation for hard-luck shrimpers to make "easy money." After all, many of his subjects were friends. "I'm turning it into a novel," he announced, explaining that he could now tell the story with composite characters and fictional names. In all, he interviewed more than a dozen drug runners and law enforcement officials, and spent long periods on the decks of shrimp boats at sea. Almost twenty-five years later, *Potluck* was published.

"At one point, I was worried that the plot and scenes were too outlandish," he told me, "but a former drug smuggler and the local sheriff assured me that everything I mentioned in the book had been tried. Immediately after the book came out, people around here were snapping up the books like mad, trying to figure out who my characters resembled in real life."

St. Petersburg Times reporter Lucy Morgan helped to break the story about Big Bend drug running in the early 1980s. "I was working on a story about the ineffectiveness of the statewide grand jury—which was created at [then Florida governor] Reubin Askew's urging to deal with drug smuggling—and almost everyone I interviewed said I needed to be spending time in Dixie and Taylor counties," she said. "Cops who worked drug cases said they were frequently followed by green and white deputy cars within minutes of arriving in the area; the Dixie County Commission had traveled to another county to defend a drug smuggler, saying it would be an economic threat to the county if he was jailed, etc. So I decided to spend time looking at the situation. I wrote a series of stories that began running in April 1981 and continued on and off through '82 and more sporadically afterwards. The feds redesigned the district so Dixie County was shifted into the Northern District of Florida for drug prosecutions and they arrested more than 250 people."

According to Lucy, those arrested included the chief deputy in Dixie County, a former school board chairman from Dixie County, the chairman of the Taylor County Commission, the Taylor County sheriff, and other well-known people in the area. "Essentially they were providing the boats to off-load larger boats carrying thousands of pounds of marijuana," she said, "and in the later years, cocaine."

Lucy's journalistic sleuthing was not without risk. "I had any number of threats," she said, "but more often the people I was interviewing were threatened—sometimes while I was at their house doing the interviews. FDLE [Florida Department of Law Enforcement] once monitored a conversation among the smugglers in Tarpon Springs when they discussed whether it would be feasible to kill me because I had really screwed up the off-load sites on the west coast. They concluded it wouldn't be worth the uproar it would cause.

"I frequently got calls asking me to meet someone with a hot tip on the Steinhatchee River bridge at midnight, things like that. I always countered with 'How about the courthouse steps at noon?' The good ol' boys often twirled their guns as I walked by them—it was great sport. I always thought it was an advantage being a woman in those situations; most of those people would be slow to hit a woman."

While Lucy survived the ordeal to become the Tallahassee bureau chief for the *St. Petersburg Times*, many of the *Times'* green metal distribution boxes found a new use—as artificial reefs. Some say they can still spot them at the bottom of the Gulf, collecting barnacles.

Of course, drug smuggling hasn't completely disappeared. In 2004, a fisherman told me he had seen another fisherman find six bales of cocaine floating in the water near St. Marks. "Five were liquid," he said, "but one was completely dry. He got so excited that he just ran his boat up on the ramp, no trailer or nothing. That one bale was worth at least sixty-five thousand dollars."

Some have found long-lasting fortune along the Big Bend coast. For others, the taste has been fleeting. For Liz and me, paddling along the pristine islands and marshes, richness could not be measured. We were pirates only in a childlike sense, fellow travelers on a journey of discovery.

12

FRAGILE EXISTENCE

Liz and I cruised past Pepperfish Keys, islands of marsh, sand, and occasional palms. They host rookeries for pelicans, cormorants, ibis, and other birds. "I've seen these covered with white pelicans in the winter," said Liz. Most of the birds gather on the Gulf side of the islands, where there are open beaches and numerous rocks for perching. We tried to give them a wide berth, but we still spooked several flocks.

My friend Julie Brashears, coordinator for the Great Florida Birding Trail, became excited when she learned of my kayaking trip. She called the Big Bend coast "one of Florida's last great birding adventures." She described birds that might be spotted—white pelicans, black-bellied and piping plovers, willets, short- and long-billed dowitchers, marbled godwits, dunlins, greater and lesser yellowlegs, common and red-throated loons, and rafts of wintering diving and dabbling ducks. "Rarities like vermilion flycatchers, western kingbirds and golden eagles wouldn't surprise me, even groove-billed anis from Texas," she said, "but terrestrial access is limited, so birding this area by kayak makes sense."

Bald eagles, once endangered, are increasingly common along the coast, and graceful swallow-tailed kites often soar overhead in spring and summer. Estuarine marshes in this region are one of the last holdouts in the state for elusive black rails, which skulk below rare wintering sparrows like Nelson's sharp-tailed, saltmarsh sharp-tailed, and seaside.

Julie also stressed that the Big Bend coast is the jumping-off point in fall and the first land in spring for many trans-Gulf migrants. "In October and April, you can listen at night for the chirping of songbirds flying overhead,

The Big Bend coast has been called "one of Florida's last great birding adventures." Here, a group of shorebirds feed along Hagen's Cove, between Steinhatchee and Keaton Beach. It is one of only a handful of coastal access points easily reached by vehicle.

giving contact calls to keep their flocks together in the darkness," she said. "During the spring bird migration, exhausted palm warblers often land on boats in the Gulf to rest."

As the kayaking trail becomes popular, I wondered if migrating birds would land on kayaks as well, just like butterflies and dragonflies had landed on my boat. Many of the birds have flown 600 miles nonstop across the Gulf at an average of 15 to 45 miles per hour. Some beat their wings more than a million times without stopping. Fat reserves and muscle mass can both be used up, especially if the birds battle headwinds. Weakened and hungry, they rest and refuel in pockets of good shoreline habitat before spreading out across North America. That's where wild areas like the Big Bend coast can prove vital to their survival.

Since many of the birds fly at night at high altitudes, scientists are employing Doppler radar, normally used to view thunderstorms, to track their movements and to identify key stopover habitat along the Gulf. While much of the Big Bend coast is protected, many important stopover habitats have been converted to condominiums and beachfront homes along other parts of the Gulf, contributing to an overall decline in many migratory species over the past thirty years. Some scientists suggest that the number of birds crossing the Gulf each spring has dropped by more than half since the 1960s, an alarming figure. Groups such as the Nature Conservancy are purchasing key shoreline areas, especially west of the Big Bend, before it is too late.

The plight of migratory birds was brought home to me when I witnessed a springtime banding of migratory songbirds. Mist nets were set up along a hardwood hammock just before dawn. A white-eyed vireo, two catbirds, and a northern parula warbler were caught. One of the bird banders blew on a catbird's belly to see if there was a nesting pouch to indicate a female, or whether there were fat reserves. "See, this one has been here feeding for a couple of days," he said, showing me yellow fat reserves. Another bird had no visible fat reserves. "He probably just came in from flying across the Gulf. Sometimes we'll suddenly get fifty or sixty birds hit the mist net at one time. We call that the Yucatán Express."

The captured birds were measured, weighed, and marked with small metal leg bands. Each band bore a different number that would be recorded on an international registry. Banding helps to determine the migratory patterns of specific bird species. "We've found birds we've banded the year before in the very same spot," said one of the volunteer banders. "People say that if you develop an area, the birds will simply move over, but that's not necessarily true. They seem programmed to return to the same places."

Liz and I left Pepperfish Keys and began paddling the six-mile span of open water to Horseshoe Beach. The water was turbid, the wind against us. "We should call this Monotony Bay," said Liz. I tried some fishing. Fish were jumping everywhere, but none took my lure.

"I need live shrimp or cut bait," I called to Liz.

"Whatever you say, Captain," she said, smiling. I had envisioned catching fresh fish for our dinners but hadn't produced any thus far, and here it was the second-to-last day. I also wondered what to do with a fish once I caught it before we were ready to camp. I had no cooler, so if I wanted to keep the fish for dinner, I would have to put in on a stringer. However, I had heard of one kayak fisherman who put a redfish on a stringer and was trailed for miles by a persistent shark. Finally, he had to release the fish.

I was mindful that some trout fishermen had caught a 14-foot bull shark near Pepperfish Keys not that long before. They lassoed the beast and towed it into shore. The shark weighed a whopping 626 pounds, and its stomach

A thunderstorm approaches the natural beach of Hagen's Cove, between Steinhatchee and Keaton Beach. We had one scare from a storm but otherwise enjoyed clear weather.

contents turned up two horseshoe crabs, a seagull, and an assortment of fish, but no kayaks.

Sea kayaker Ken Johnson of Corpus Christi, Texas, almost became shark bait when he was paddling around Cumberland Island, Georgia, in 1999. He was rounding the northern end of the island against a headwind when he heard a rushing wake. Suddenly his kayak was knocked 30 degrees off course. Startled, he quickly paddled to shore and examined his craft. He found teeth marks, scratches, and a large shark's tooth sticking out of the hull of his kayak. A marine biologist believed the tooth had belonged to a mako shark. So, even though Johnson's boat was blue and white, and mine was yellow, I believe I made a wise decision not to use a stringer for any fish I caught.

A distant thunderstorm livened things up. Ominous booms of thunder echoed across the water. I suddenly felt small. We were a mile or more offshore, with only salt marsh to our left. The town of Horseshoe Beach was a distant five or more miles on the horizon. We could only move forward.

A year before, I had been caught by a storm in Florida Bay—at the bottom of the Everglades—while solo canoeing. I had paddled from Flamingo into an area known as Snake Bight, intrigued by the name. Snook, redfish, crocodiles, and even a small bull shark feeding in foot-deep water enthralled me. I spotted diving osprey and flocks of egrets, herons, and roseate spoonbills feeding along mangrove shores. My only worries were the hordes of black marsh mosquitoes that breed around mangrove roots. By paddling too close, the pesky critters quickly appointed me as their primary blood donor, ranking me down there with plankton in the Everglades/Florida Bay food chain. They hid in the boat, pestering my legs and feet. They seemed to come and go at will once they knew my position.

Aiming for a cluster of egrets and pink spoonbills, I soon learned that mosquitoes were the least of my worries. The thunderhead before me had posed little threat—moving from my left to my right across Florida Bay. What I didn't notice was the storm building up behind mangroves on the landward side. By the time I heard thunder, it was too late.

The wind suddenly gusted. Mosquitoes were blown from the boat. My canoe spun around and slammed against thick mangroves. Thunder rumbled again. The sky darkened. I was in a bit of trouble. Mosquitoes are nothing compared to lightning on open water. Avoiding lightning is basic survival, and I was being wedged between two big thunderheads.

Solo paddling back to Flamingo against gusty winds required a monumental effort. Wading birds disappeared into thickets; only the ospreys continued whistling. Perched on high branches, they watched my painstakingly slow retreat to safety.

The red mangroves offered little refuge. Since their feet were immersed in water, there was no dry land in sight, and their thick prop roots made passage nearly impossible. My only real alternative was to keep paddling and try to outrun the storm, an inch at a time.

I struggled out of Snake Bight, paddling mightily, all the while trying to keep the bow from being blown into mangroves again. I finally rounded the curve between Joe Kemp Key and Christian Point. The wind was suddenly in my favor. I nearly collapsed with relief.

When I neared the marina, the weather miraculously calmed. Only a light rain fell. Swallows swooped in to feed on mosquitoes. I sighed. All had returned to normal in Florida Bay.

Now, on a different stretch of coast, trying to outrace a storm across Monotony Bay, my boat felt like a slow-moving barge. It is difficult to paddle a fully-loaded sea kayak faster than 3 miles per hour, at least the model I had.

As the sky darkened, I felt I was losing the race to outrun the storm. Maybe my Florida Bay luck had run out, I thought. Any moment I expected to be overcome by strong winds and pelted with rain, providing a challenging test for my tiny craft and newly honed kayaking skills. Once again, lightning was my main worry, a primal fear. As I was growing up, my mother used to tell us about how her grandfather had been caught by a storm while wandering the wide-open Indiana Dunes. A split-second lightning bolt cost him his life at age fifty-three.

About a half mile from Horseshoe Beach, the storm passed just to the west. Another miracle. Maybe great-grandfather was watching out for us.

Horseshoe Beach County Campground was a Spartan place with no trees or trash receptacles, and dirty bathrooms. The centerpiece was a busy public landing with the fumes, noise, and frustrations commonly associated with boats that are either working or refusing to work.

We walked a half mile to a convenience store to buy a cold drink and read the same type of depressing headline news we had read before our trip. The Middle East violence seemed far away, remote, and bizarre, yet, on some level, I felt it. I can't explain how. Maybe humanity is part of one big organism called earth and we can sense what another branch of our species is doing. I was eager to start paddling again. Even though we had narrowly missed a storm, I felt less vulnerable on the water than I did sitting in front of that convenience store reading the newspaper. We quickly ate our dripping ice-cream bars and walked back to the landing.

As we approached our evening destination—Butler Island—Liz and I kept our gaze fixed on a huge billowing cloud before us. Early evening light tinged it pink. "I swear," said Liz, "that looks like one big poodle."

"It sure does," I agreed. Suddenly, the back of my kayak lifted up and a huge manatee exploded from underneath. My first thought was that I had encountered a whale. I scrambled to steady myself. From poodles to manatees, this coast can really surprise you, I thought.

In the turbid water, I hadn't seen the manatee, and he must not have seen me. Manatees are surprisingly quick when startled. "There's a manatee on the Wakulla River that purposely tips over canoes," said Liz.

"Maybe it's the same one, heading south before cold weather hits," I replied, scanning the water for signs of a torpedolike return.

Manatees are Florida's gentle giants, often called sea cows because they graze on voluminous amounts of sea grass and water weeds. This can give

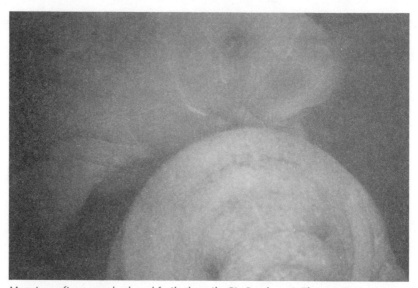

Manatees often move back and forth along the Big Bend coast. They venture up rivers in warm months and seek refuge in constant-temperature springs in winter, especially along the Suwannee and at Crystal River. These manatees were frequenting the Wakulla River in July.

them enormous amounts of gas, too; those bubbles rising up through the water are not just exhalations of carbon dioxide. I've had to hold my nose while paddling over a manatee pod on the Wakulla River.

Manatees often move back and forth along the coast. They venture up Big Bend rivers such as the St. Marks and Wakulla in warm months and seek refuge in constant temperature springs in winter, especially along the Suwannee and at Crystal River. They also enjoy the warm effluent of power plants.

Red tide and sudden cold snaps are major causes of death, but people driving high-powered boats kill scores of manatees each year for a total of 1,237 verified deaths from 1974 through 2003. Florida has almost one million registered powerboats, and slightly more than three thousand manatees. Through the eons of their evolution, they've never had to flee large, threatening objects swiftly moving across the surface. Now they do. When a boat approaches, manatees generally dive and move away, flipping up their powerful tails. This is why their tails and lower backs are the body parts most often struck by boats. While about half of boat-related manatee deaths are attributed to blunt trauma from a collision, almost all manatees have propeller scars. Many sea cows that return year after year to various fresh-water springs and power plants can be identified by them.

In 2002, I had a sobering assignment for *Florida Wildlife* magazine: write about the animal rehabilitation facilities at Orlando's SeaWorld theme park. At first, I had been excited—a free trip to Florida's most educational theme park where it normally costs fifty bucks just to walk in the gate. But when I journeyed behind the scenes, beyond the glitz and glitter and mobs of visitors flocking to pet dolphins and snap pictures of Shamu, my mood quickly changed. Members of the SeaWorld veterinary services staff were draining gallons of fluid from the chest cavity of a large manatee. A boat had struck the sea cow about three months earlier. Bloated and near death from internal injuries and a gaping hole in her side, the SeaWorld animal rescue team captured the half-ton sirenian and brought her to their rehabilitation facility. Once stabilized, the draining procedure was an everyday occurrence.

While watching, I began to feel queasy, not so much from the voluminous amounts of pus, but because I knew the animal was in pain. She winced, her normally placid face scrunched up. If manatees could scream, this one would have been howling. On behalf of our species, I felt guilty. Florida is one of the fastest-growing states in the country; there seems no end to the unbridled growth. The Sunshine State's 2002 population of more than 16 million people may double by the year 2030, reaching a population in excess of 33 million. Will the number of boats double as well?

Dr. Mike Walsh, director of veterinary services, stepped back from the manatee and tilted his head toward me, all the while keenly observing the procedure. "If this were you or I we'd probably be laying in a hospital bed with bandages on," he said. "We certainly wouldn't be surrounded by water. That's a major complication, but we've worked out a system to where we can treat the wound and avoid getting it contaminated; it is almost watertight."

As the staff sterilized and bandaged the wound, Dr. Walsh explained that they were using something called tegaderm, used with humans for bedsores. They adapted it to manatees and sea turtles, super-gluing it over wounds that have dressing on them. Another innovation was the circular platform that the manatee was lying on. It was perforated and could be mechanically lowered or raised inside the water tank. This reduced the need to frequently capture and immobilize an animal for treatment, thus reducing treatment time and stress for the animal.

Once the manatee was fitted with a Velcro jacket to help keep her afloat and to insulate the bandage, she was lowered into the water. Immediately, she swam up to the edge of the pool and stuck her head out in a friendly gesture. Forgiveness, I thought, from pain to forgiveness. Then she began munching on floating lettuce. A healthy appetite, that was a good sign.

Dr. Walsh led me to the "orphan tank." This was where baby manatees were kept who had been abandoned or whose mothers died. Two manatees about the size of large pillows let me rub them under their chins and on their bellies. They suckled my fingers. This was the melt-your-heart tank, I thought. "Now, what is there not to love about a manatee?" said a smiling Dr. Walsh, as if reading my mind. He didn't need to convince me.

"We know now that we can take an orphan at two days of age and get him back out in the wild successfully. It's great we know that now. It's not good enough to have them do well in an aquarium and then think that in twenty years you're going to reintroduce them into the wild. You've got to have that available from the start. That's where Florida has been way ahead on this species."

Like manatees, sea turtles are also injured by boats, something I had not realized before my visit. "Sea turtles can take a lot of punishment," said Dr. Walsh. "We have a number of turtles where the prop has sliced right through their spinal cord. They're basically paralyzed, paraplegic, but we're able to maintain them as long as they're in a protected environment. We also see some natural disease problems and entanglements with fishing hooks, crab traps, and monofilament line like we do with the manatee. It's interesting that they share so many of the same difficulties."

According to Dr. Walsh, turtle shells were once repaired with substances like bondo or fiberglass, the "hard patch" approach. Since the shell is a vibrant part of the turtle's body, this repair method did not allow the wound to properly heal. In the past decade, Walsh and his team developed a type of flexible wet bandaging material, similar to what is used on manatees. The wound can then be cleaned on a regular basis.

Having a state-of-the-art laboratory on site also helps the vet staff with timely X-rays, ultrasounds, blood work, serum chemistries, and cultures. Dr. Walsh showed me a nifty heat-sensitive camera that can detect inflammations and infections at a distance of several feet, a clear advantage when working with animals such as polar bears. But despite the technological breakthroughs, Dr. Walsh still stressed prevention, especially regarding manatees and sea turtles.

"They just weren't evolved to take on fast boats," he said. "They [the animals] become habituated to the fact that there's a boat, but if a boat is coming too fast, there's no time to react before they're hit. So if people slow down and give them time, they'll get out of the way.

"We can help a lot of them [injured animals]. We've figured out a lot of techniques, but it's the boat speeds that are important. It's the protection zones that are important, and it's the general population agreeing to give them a chance to work; that's what's going to make the difference. Boats and manatees can coexist."

I felt fortunate that my encounter with a wild manatee along the Big Bend coast involved a plastic kayak with no propeller.

Butler Island was remote, scenic, and buggy. Liz and I heated water for our last freeze-dried dinner over a smoky fire. As choking clouds of no-see-ums emerged, we sat huddled over a small battery-operated tent fan, eating from the same pot, dripping sweat, and swatting bugs. This last night on the trail was hot and miserable, yet it was still wonderful to sit under mature cedars and watch huge redfish swim into inches-deep water to feed. We slept beside Indian shell middens, natural trash heaps deposited by early native people who had lived or camped on this island for generations.

The largest midden in the area is near Cedar Key. Built over a 3,500-year period, it stands 28 feet tall and covers a whopping 5 acres. I cannot even imagine how many meals the sea provided those early inhabitants. One time when I felt confused, I sat on top of that huge mound overlooking the Gulf. I lay on a bench and breathed in the salt air as the wind whispered across gleaming white shells and mature cedars and live oaks. After a long while, I began to feel clearer, with a renewed sense of purpose and vigor. Finding stillness helped, and so did that ancient, long-used spot.

Leaving our no-see-um friends in the morning, we paddled across Horseshoe Cove through an eerie maze of exposed oyster bars, black against the rising sun and silvery sea. In between the bars, schools of speckled trout churned the water in feeding frenzies. Small baitfish leapt out of the water in desperate attempts to escape. In the distance, we spotted dolphin fins slicing through the water. Dolphins, too, were enjoying the rich bounties of this place.

Nearing the Suwannee River, we passed the Caribbean-looking island of Big Pine with its white-sand beaches and numerous sabal palms. It was part of the 53,000-acre Lower Suwannee National Wildlife Refuge. The refuge covers the mouth and more than 20 miles of the famed 325-mile Suwannee River, made famous by Stephen Foster's "Old Folks at Home." The Suwannee Sound is one of the largest undeveloped river delta-estuarine systems remaining in the United States and a major wildlife haven. More than 250 bird species, 90 of which are known to nest on the refuge, have been recorded.

As we paddled the sound's dark waters, we hoped to glimpse the dramatic leaps of Gulf sturgeon, a primitive species that first emerged from the Jurassic period, about 195 million years ago. In the spring, these fish—federally designated as threatened—migrate from the Gulf to the Suwannee River for spawning, where they remain all summer. On rare occasions, a leaping Gulf sturgeon, which can weigh up to 250 pounds, has knocked people out of boats.

We stopped at the treeless Coon Island and visited the ruins of a fish camp that had been destroyed by a storm. Once again, we were reminded that this coast was not only to be appreciated for its tremendous beauty but also to be respected for its awesome power. And though people seek to establish firm footholds with their buildings and docks, they are no real match for the occasional fury of storms or the persistent rise of sea water.

About two miles from the town of Suwannee, the wind kicked up and hit us broadside. Waves washed over my bow. I became nervous and a bit agitated. Here it was the end of our trip and I could become shark bait! I tried to relax and roll with the waves. It seemed to be a reminder that this coast can kick your butt anytime. It did not invite respect—it demanded it.

Once we turned into the main channel toward Suwannee, the wind was finally at our backs. The landing was a welcome sight, despite the water moccasin that someone had killed and left along the shore. As we packed our gear, we met four grizzled fishermen loading their boat. "How far you been coming?" asked a man.

"We put in at the Aucilla River, nine days ago," I replied.

"Nine days," he drawled. "Damn, I wouldn't be able to paddle that thing in my swimming pool without tipping over!"

We ate gobs of steamed shrimp and vegetables at the Salt Creek Restaurant, followed by mud pie. Perfect. Jerrie Lindsey, our friend and supervisor, arrived to pick us up. She didn't sit too close. We needed showers. We posed for photos beside our boats, and then it was time to leave. The Big Bend coast would be there for future adventures, I knew. We had made a wise investment to protect most of her shores, yet she was still fragile in many ways. We needed to heed the lessons of Florida Bay and the Everglades, where attempts to repair past abuse will run into the billions. I gave my silent thanks, vowing to return.

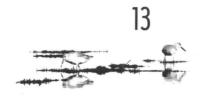

13

SIMPLE LIFE

After Liz and I finished our kayaking expedition, we returned that winter to the town of Suwannee to do a presentation on the paddling trail at the local chamber of commerce. About eighty people showed up, most of them retirees who had recently relocated to Suwannee.

"About eight hundred people live in Suwannee," explained one resident, "but only four hundred are full-time. Most are weekenders. Only 15 percent or so are native to this area. Most are retirees; we have only ten or twelve kids in the whole community. They have to go to school in Old Town or Chiefland." The woman pointed out that taxes and property values are going up exponentially, a story we had heard all along the coast.

Another woman explained that the nearest grocery store of any size was in Old Town, about 23 miles away, or at the Super Wal-Mart in Chiefland, 37 miles away. "If you want to do other kinds of shopping, you have to drive to Gainesville, 67 miles away." She had all the mileage figures memorized.

That evening, the group served up chili and crackers, along with a dessert buffet. They also brought food to several in the community who were "shut-ins" or "just too ornery to get out and socialize."

After our presentation, a middle-aged man approached who introduced himself as Preston Chavous. I've already shared some of his pirate and smuggling stories. Soft-spoken, Preston asked if we had seen signs of steamboats that had sunk almost a century before at the mouth of Cow Creek near Sink Creek, and at Boiler Pass along the Suwannee. We shook our heads. I had no idea they were there. "My mother's family goes back eight generations along this coast," he said. "I have the original map of Suwannee, the first one, laid out by my uncle. I live up the road and have a log cabin built in 1863. Come see me." He gave me his card. It read, "Munden Camp." I promised I would. Here was an eighth-generation native among a burgeoning population of newcomers. I wanted to learn about his perspective.

The following week, I called Preston Chavous. After the Suwannee presentation, curiosity had been gnawing at me. "Come on over," he said politely over the phone. He gave me directions from Old Town.

As I turned into Munden Camp, I was struck by its picturesque scenery. Huge hardwood trees encircled a cluster of small houses and trailers. A tree-lined canal led to the lower Suwannee River. In the camp's center was the ancient log cabin, situated behind a split-rail fence. No lights shone through the windows, so I knocked on the door of an adjacent shotgun-style house, one that also appeared to have some age. A faded Coke machine stood on the front porch, slightly tilted. Preston came to the door and greeted me warmly. He led me through a kitchen sided with plank boards and adorned with real wood furniture. "This place was built in 1925," he said. "This is old Florida."

We sat in a small living room and talked, though I did most of the listening. Preston had an encyclopedic mind when it came to family and area history. For him, the two were tightly interwoven.

"I grew up in Old Town," he said. "My mother was born in the Lime Sinks; my grandmother was born in Cow Creek; my great-grandmother was born at Fishbone in 1855. They [great-grandparents] poled to Atsena Otie Key [near present-day Cedar Key] to get their mail."

Preston rattled off dates and the names of people and places. He talked about early steamships, railroads, and logging. He talked about life before electricity and modern roads and conveniences. It was difficult to keep up, and I began to wonder how and why this man carried the history of nearly forgotten generations. He had the memories of someone many years older than his fifty-six years. I put my curiosity into the form of a question; Preston paused before answering. "I was a sickly child, and I grew up with old people," he began. "My grandma poked a lot of this stuff in me. She poked every bit in me that she could, and I could remember it. And I got to researching this stuff as a child at ten, twelve, thirteen years old. My grandmother was basically an uneducated woman who had to raise a family by herself in the '20s. Grandfather died in '25.

"We were poor people, simple people, we lived in simple worlds. We weren't ignorant. We read daily. From the time we were small we read the newspaper. We read every periodical we could get our hands on. Of course, I was always ambitious and I liked politics, and I liked people well. My family, they weren't highly educated, but they were smart, and they made damn sure that I got an education. I have a bachelor's plus. I taught school, I was the coach at the prison for five years, and then I owned a title company."

Preston said he moved out of the area at one point and "made monster money" in his title business, but he quickly learned that money didn't equate with happiness. "The lack of money was sometimes a big problem," he said, "but too much of it was a damn big problem. And that's very true with most people." He returned home to set up his title business locally. He eventually bought several tracts of land in the town of Suwannee, but he came upon hard times. "I pissed a bunch of people off because I sold it [the land]," he said, "but I would have ended up walking out of town if I hadn't. All of a sudden we got all these people moving in."

He sighed. The heavy growth in the area was a trend he clearly wished he could have steered in a different direction. Viewing the change from such an age-old spot must have made it worse. "I don't know what motivates me to remember all this," he continued, returning to my question. "This guy called me last year and we talked for three hours on the phone about my mother's side of the family. He asked me if I had it on computer, and I said it's in my brain. Then he came over here, and he was just amazed at all the stuff that I had."

He paused again before continuing. "I have no children," he said. "I've never been married. I'm not warped, not crazy, not stupid. Most people think if you ain't married you're stupid or crazy or dumb or something is bad wrong with you, you got a sex problem or something. No I don't have that. I have a diabetes problem. I have about a half-foot on one foot, and have three toes on the other, and I've drunk enough Jack Daniels to kill me and you and four more. Most of my friends tell me I should be rich. I don't really care about being rich. I like people too much to be rich."

He glanced outside. Sunlight was fading and I could feel cold air creeping through the walls. "So, you want to see the cabin?" he asked.

"You bet." I was curious how area pioneers lived; I had an inkling the cabin would give me clues. Historic buildings and objects can be guideposts for understanding the past.

Preston Chavous of Munden Camp, near the town of Suwannee, stands before the wood-frame porch of his 1863 log cabin. "This house has been kind of my charm," he said. "It's full of memorabilia."

"I've restored the old cabin, a little too good, probably," Preston said as we swung open a creaky screen door and stepped onto a porch. "This house has kind of been my charm. It's full of memorabilia, let me assure you." I admired a fishing net hanging on the porch wall, one adorned with antique fishing lures. A jumble of decades-old rods and reels leaned in a corner as if placed there fifty years before and never touched since. "I have a good collection of fishing stuff," he commented matter-of-factly.

As he opened the main door, the smell of real wood gave me a nostalgic feeling of visiting old fishing cabins as a child. Except for the framing, few houses today are made of real wood. "Smells good, don't it?" he said. I nodded appreciatively. It was the smell of old Florida.

I gazed wondrously around the cabin. It was like an antique store with no price tags, or a museum without interpretive panels. Every small nook harbored some relic of the past. Preston, wearing a bright orange sweatshirt, seemed to glow against the dark wood and shadows, like a brightly colored moth. He touched one of the logs that had been notched and stacked atop each other almost a century and a half before.

"The logs are cypress, Doug. They're original. Only one log got wet; the rest are in good shape. The fireplace has been redone, though. Originally it was clay and moss and sticks. That clay was baked. I can remember going in a lot of old houses when I was young and you could see the old clay chimneys. That was fifty years ago. Those houses have been gone for some time now. I know of one still left. This one [brick chimney] was probably built in the 1920s."

I yearned for the warmth of a crackling fire, but I knew we wouldn't be inside long enough to really benefit from it. In my own house south of Tallahassee, we have a wood stove, and I enjoy the whole process of cutting and chopping wood. A wood fire is a basic and direct heat source. We also have real wood on the inside walls, planks that I planed myself from rough-cut juniper. After driving home through rush-hour traffic, the simplicity of my home helps put me at ease. Perhaps that's the central purpose of a home.

Preston pointed to an antique wood desk in a corner. "That came from Cedar Key," he said. A black manual typewriter rested on top. "And I got my uncle's typewriter."

He moved to a wall, reached up and took down a framed hand-drawn map. "This is the original map of Suwannee. It was made in '23 by my uncle. Only about eight homesteads were platted." It was difficult to imagine the tiny town when compared to today's Suwannee, with several hundred houses spaced tightly together along a maze of canals.

He walked to a bookshelf filled with stacks of folded yellowed newspapers. "I have a good collection of newspapers, the *Dixie County Advocate*," he said, reaching for a paper. "My folks started it. I have them all from the first one to 1961. Let's see what this one says, 'Dixie Highway Soon to be Completed,' 1929." He carefully refolded the paper and put it back. "You have to be really careful with this stuff."

The tour continued. He pointed to a framed letter. "That's from the governor of Georgia after he stayed in Suwannee." Nodding to another photo, he said: "That's Payne's Prairie. My cousins owned it. You can't see it very good. Isn't it beautiful? Nineteen thirteen that picture is." I had often visited Payne's Prairie near Gainesville; it is now a popular state park that harbors a herd of reintroduced bison. But more often than not I whiz through the prairie on Interstate 75.

We walked toward the bedroom where an antique oak bed filled up most of the room. Preston purchased it from an estate in Cedar Key, he said. He pointed to a black and brown steamer's trunk at the foot of the quilt-covered mattress. "This was my great-grandfather's trunk," he said. "I had the damn thing restored. It's full of letters—I get in there and read them once in a while. I've got an original Coke tray in there. And I got a bunch of the old, old marbles. They were my grandmother's."

We returned to the living room. It was good to keep moving because the temperature was dropping. Preston pointed to wide cypress boards resting on rafters. "Those boards Daddy was going to build a boat out of in '53, and he never built it," he explained. He pointed to another spot in the rafters. "And that's quilting frames. You probably know what those are."

I nodded toward the front door, solid wood with a round porthole in the middle. "Is that original?" I asked.

Preston laughed. "No, my friend made that for the Salt Creek Restaurant. We probably couldn't register this place for the national historic register of homes, but that's not really important to me. This place is just neat, Doug. It's neat to me."

He pointed to a row of dark clothes irons near the fireplace, the kind people used to heat up beside a fire or on a wood stove. "I know you never did no ironing," he said.

"Not like that."

Hanging beside the fireplace was a tangle of copper tubes attached to a metal container. "That's my great-uncle's moonshine still. It was in the woods. I went and found it when I grew up, and I toted it out and kept it." I had never actually seen a still in operation and wondered how the contraption worked. I was sure Preston knew how, but I didn't ask. There was more to see, and my brain could only take in so much at one time. Now I knew what Preston meant when he said his grandmother "poked" information into him.

From the fireplace mantle, Preston reached for a collection of home-made turkey callers, most carved out of cedar. He let me turn one over in my hands. I had never hunted turkey, but I understood that it required a high level of skill to be successful. During the spring mating season, a caller would imitate a male turkey. It would attract other males, who viewed the caller as a threat.

We walked to an oak cabinet, one with antique glass doors. "This is filled with early political history, from '13 to '48," said Preston, "and legal papers from everything from Governor John Martin to LeRoy Collins. They were old friends of my uncle's."

He spoke to me about Florida governor LeRoy Collins, who helped to usher in the civil rights era during his administration in the 1960s, and about growing up with African-Americans in Old Town. "They weren't black to me, Doug; they were about like my aunts and uncles. They came to our house. Most of them [blacks] from Old Town that see me and meet me on the street, they say, 'Hey Cousin Preston!' . . . We cohabitate well around each other. There's none that live on the coast; they come here very frequently, though. There's a lot of blacks that fish out of here."

"But why don't they live on the coast?" I asked. Liz and I had rarely seen an African-American in coastal towns along the kayaking trail.

"Because of starvation," he said. "The coast was a rough area, Doug. People came here to hide and stuff. There was no work if you didn't fish. The interior was logging and farming, and they [blacks] worked. Most of them were honorable people, and some of their children ended up very well in this world. Not simple. Not very simple whatsoever."

Preston showed me a faded black-and-white photograph of people standing before the cabin. "That's the camp, Doug, in the '40s," he said. "You can't see it good, but that's it. Used to be a lot of pear trees here, Doug. The old folks would pole in here on the creek and pick the pears and take them home and can them in the summertime. Granny Oldund said she was doing that in '15 and '16. She'd come up the river and pole herself up here and pick these pears and then she'd take them back home and can them. Can you imagine? Would a woman do that today, Doug?" He laughed loudly.

I felt a twinge of guilt. I have a sand pear tree in my yard that produces voluminous amounts of hard-skinned pears. They make great pear sauce or preserves, but my family always seems too busy to cook them. Every summer, they rot on the ground and feed the worms and flies, wastefulness my rural forebearers wouldn't have allowed. In the not-so-distant past, a grocery store was an abstract luxury or a place to obtain only basic necessities such as flour and coffee. People took full advantage of seasonal foods that were available.

As a boy growing up in Tallahassee, I visited a friend up the road who had recently moved from a rural area near Woodville. When I arrived, he and his family were shelling peas on the front porch, an entire bushel. I had never shelled peas. Mine came in a can or they were frozen, so I joined them, talking and shelling peas. It was simple, and it was bonding. We talked of the day's events and of people who weren't there, a bit of gossip mixed with just plain talk. I liked it.

There's nothing complicated about shelling peas, but when the hands are busy, the mind seems to relax. Perhaps early people discovered this long ago when they manipulated objects and food with their hands.

A wonderful north Florida story reveals a clue about the time and space of a people who lived in simpler times. A man approached a woman who was shelling peas on her porch. "Ma'am, do you know what time it is?" he asked.

The woman nodded, spit out a wad of tobacco snuff, and studied the afternoon shadows creeping across the rough-cut boards of her porch floor. "About a crack-and-a-half until dinner," she said, and continued shelling peas.

Preston spread out his hands as if trying to encompass the entire cabin. "I don't know who will like this stuff when I'm all gone," he said. "Maybe my nieces and nephews; they're getting inquisitive about things."

He turned toward another corner and handed me a handsome shotgun. "It's an L. C. Smith double-barreled. My grandfather got it from a group of hunters from Lakeland in 1916. He would guide them. He'd cook for them and he took them hunting, and they paid him so much a day to take them hunting in California Swamp.

"My youngest nephew, he's fifteen or sixteen, he wants that gun. What will he do with it? It's fairly valuable, but he's in a different culture, a different world than I am."

Preston pointed to a deer rack that hung from one of the log walls. "My daddy killed that deer in December of '39 in the mill branches out here in the swamp. We hunted different than what most folks do today. When we left the camp to go hunting, we left with the dogs tied to us. When we got off in the woods, we turned them loose. Nobody drove a truck. We walked and waded in the swamp. We were swamp hunters. And we loved the swamp; it was part of us and part of our heritage."

Preston paused and looked at me sadly, then glanced wistfully at the deer antlers again. I could easily picture the scene he evoked, of hunters on foot in a wet wilderness, following the distant yelps of hounds. "That style of our lives is all gone, Doug," he continued. "We don't hunt anymore. And the older daddy got, in particular, the more and more environmentally sensitive he became. He didn't classify himself as such, but if he had been a young man, he would have been a big environmentalist. As Daddy got older, he despised the timber cutting. It would bother him real bad. If he had had his way, they wouldn't have cut no more timber. They cut the oaks and that just about broke his heart. I can remember when they did that. Cedar, cypress, pine, then the oaks and the gum to make the crates with and stuff."

I've often hiked and waded through coastal swamps and found the huge stumps left by loggers. The only virgin cypress still standing were ones that were hollow or twisted, of little commercial value. The rest were second-growth trees that would take centuries to rival their predecessors, if allowed to mature and live to old age. I've often wished that people with foresight could have spared places in north Florida, like southwest Florida's Corkscrew Swamp. There, the trees dwarf people and instill an unrivaled awe. If only . . .

"This place has changed," said Preston, speaking more broadly of the entire area. "It will never go back to what it was. People are coming here unbelievably. I sold a lot of land that was developed, but I preserved a little bit of it. Maybe I might leave this damn place to the state. I don't know."

He sighed and glanced wistfully around the room before moving toward the front door. I followed him outside. Despite the chilly night air, I felt warm, richer of spirit, as if many people had shared their lives with me. "Thank you, Preston," I said, shaking his hand. There was little else to say. Preston's world was ebbing like an outgoing tide; we both knew you couldn't stop it or even slow it down, only grab a small piece and hold on tight.

14

SWAMP GARDEN

A natural garden of ferns, bright green against gray and brown trunks of cypress and gum, extended into the deep recesses of Tide Swamp. A white-tailed deer made its way down a well-worn path. Countless songbirds sang in the leafy canopy, mostly unseen. I recognized the *chick-a-per-weeoo-chick* of the white-eyed vireo and the *zweet-zweet-zweet* of the colorful prothonotary warbler but rarely caught glimpses of the birds.

Springtime had lured me to Tide Swamp. Since the paddling trip, I had been office-bound for long stretches of time, a widespread ailment in our modern society. Layers of concrete and drywall, conditioned air, and windows that don't open had insulated me from the earth's pulse; the natural environment, primarily seen through glass, almost seemed alien or Disneyesque at times. A visit to Tide Swamp—public land situated between Keaton Beach and Steinhatchee—was a welcome tonic.

Like other coastal wetlands south of Steinhatchee—Pine Log, Pocoson, and California swamps—Tide Swamp feeds vital nutrients to the Gulf and helps to ensure good water quality by filtering pollutants. The watery wilderness is also beautiful in April.

A raspy red-shouldered hawk cried before lifting off and zooming to another branch. Black and yellow swallowtail butterflies flitted among purple blossoms of the lyre-leafed sage along unpaved swamp roads. And then I encountered perhaps the most striking flower of the springtime swamp—the purple flag iris with its three long unfolded sepals and three interior petals that revealed a purple-and-white striped center. Bright yellow-orange sulfur butterflies favored these flowers, finding the open wells of nectar irre-

A natural garden of ferns, bright green against gray and brown trunks of cypress and gum, extends into the deep recesses of Tide Swamp.

sistible. They cavorted from one blossom to the other, frequently joining with each other. When a breeze kicked up, the butterflies would cling to the flowers, close their delicate wings, and sway like stiff leaves, before resuming their feeding. Down the roads and old tramways, hundreds of fluttering butterflies moved through the dappled light—corridors filled with delicate angels. What is spring without butterflies?

In the fall, I often spot monarch butterflies flitting through Big Bend woodlands, on their way to coastal shrubs and trees. After they leave their summering grounds in Canada, New England, and the Great Lakes, monarchs hug the Gulf coast on their way to central Mexico, feeding on goldenrod, lantana, and other flowering plants. They build up fat reserves while traveling roughly 50 miles per day. Labeled "international travelers" by scientists, these fall migrants are several generations removed from monarchs that overwintered in Mexico during the previous year. They must navigate thousands of miles to a location they've never visited, laying eggs on milkweed plants as they go, so that the next generation of travelers can carry on the cyclical journey.

The monarch's winter destination is the Sierra Madre Mountains of central Mexico, a site only discovered in 1976. Here they cluster together in the branches and trunks of oyamel trees. Deforestation of these rain forests, along with global climate change and fragmentation of summer habitats, threaten the stability of monarch populations. Because of their wide range, monarchs are considered a prime indicator species for the ecological health of a large geographic area.

Tide Swamp is interspersed by moving water—winding clear creeks with dark bottoms filled with brown minnows. Too shallow for a kayak or canoe, these creeks must be explored on foot. Iridescent damselflies move silently across the water's surface while noisier dragonflies feast on insects. Young frogs squeak as they leap from spongy shores. Exploring along one unnamed creek, I jumped back momentarily. An unblinking eye looked up at me, a small alligator, still as a log. Perhaps I was the first human it had seen.

The swamp's interior waterways, often framed by ferns and cypress knees, do not carve their way through the land like mountain streams. Instead, they move slowly, unhurried, as if only allowed quiet passage. The creeks find their way to the Gulf, while the swamp draws sustenance from life-giving arteries.

John Muir, the great naturalist and founder of the Sierra Club, briefly became lost in a Big Bend coastal swamp on his 1,000-mile walk to the Gulf in 1867. At first, he was enchanted while wandering through a thick sabal palm forest:

> What a landscape! Only palms as far as the eye could reach! Smooth pillars rising from the grass, each capped with a sphere of leaves, shining in the sun as bright as a star. The silence and calm were as deep as ever I found in the dark, solemn pine woods of Canada, and that contentment which is an attribute of the best of God's plant people was as impressively felt in this alligator wilderness as in the homes of the happy, healthy people of the North.

After drifting "incautiously," Muir had trouble finding the return trail in the lengthening shadows of an October afternoon. His admiring prose quickly changed to a tone of desperation.

> At length, after miles of wading and wallowing, I arrived at the grand cat-brier encampment which guarded the whole forest in solid phalanx, unmeasured miles up and down across my way. Alas! The trail by which I had crossed in the morning was not to be found, and night was near. In vain I scrambled back and forth in search of an opening. There was not even a strip of dry ground on which to rest. Everywhere the long briers arched over to the vines and bushes of the watery swamp, leaving no standing-ground between them. I began to think of building some sort of a scaffold in a tree to rest on through the night, but concluded to make one more desperate effort to find the narrow track.
>
> After calm, concentrated recollection of my course, I made a long exploration toward the left of the brier line, and after scrambling a mile or so, perspiring and bleeding, I discovered the blessed trail and escaped to dry land and the light.

If Muir wandered through Tide Swamp today, he'd find his share of entanglements, but he likely would have found his way more easily. A network of roads runs through the area; the longest roadless expanse is about two miles long. And Muir would surely have bemoaned the massive cypress stumps that punctuate the swamp. The waist-high stumps are flat on top where huge crosscut saws severed their trunks nearly a century earlier. Often small trees have taken root in the slowly rotting wood.

The stumps are Tide Swamp's ghosts, relics of the virgin cypress that once towered over land and water. Some trees reached lofty heights up to 150 feet, with buttressed bases of 30 feet or more in circumference. One can only imagine their majesty.

I once visited Florida's champion bald cypress, "the Senator" in Longwood, and gazed wondrously at its 35-foot girth. Only California's redwoods instilled a similar sense of awe. The national champion bald cypress in Louisiana boasts a whopping 53-foot circumference. The fact that any such tree escaped the country's voracious appetite for cypress wood is miraculous.

Logging of the Big Bend's cypress forests began in earnest in the 1910s and continued into the 1940s, when the last of the cypress giants were felled. The ivory-billed woodpecker, a species dependent upon old-growth cypress, disappeared with them. Alexander Wilson, a Bartram-era naturalist, described the ivory-billed: "In these almost inaccessible recesses, amid ruinous piles of impending timber, his trumpet-like note and loud strokes resound through the solitary savage wilds, of which he seems the sole lord and inhabitat."

Bright green and yellow Carolina parakeets also frequented the cypress swamps. Naturalist John James Audubon described these colorful, now-extinct birds: "The richness of their plumage, their beautiful mode of flight, and even their scream, afford welcome intimation that our darkest forests and most sequestered swamps are not destitute of charms."

In a Perry newspaper interview, Charles "Buster" Borkland recalled what Taylor County was like when he arrived in 1919 to work for the Brooks-Scanlon Lumber Company. "There were miles and miles of trees never touched by the ax," he said. "This county was like a park. I can still remember the wind in the trees, with the sunlight filtering through the branches. . . . And the woods were full of game. Sometimes we'd hear panthers prowling in the woods when we went out in the early morning."

In those early, prelogging days, cypress giants dominated Tide Swamp, casting a thick veil of shade in the growing season. Smaller trees and dormant seeds seemingly waited in anticipation for one of the larger trees to fall from a storm, lightning, or old age. Then they hastened to flourish in the new window of light.

The first step in cypress logging was for a crew to clear the ground for other workers. A surveyor then sectioned off the area and planned the operation, often doing a rough calculation of board feet. A crew girdled each mature tree by notching around the base so the sap would run down, starving the trunk. While these girdled trees "seasoned," a grid of raised rail beds or trams was built by draglines that scooped up the wet earth. Hardwood trees were cut and laid parallel along the beds, and cypress crossties were hammered into place. Steel rails were then anchored to this base with iron spikes.

"Sand cars" moved down the rails, dumping sand to fill in gaps and stabilize the rails. When the trams were in place, cutting crews walked or waded into the swamp and felled the girdled cypresses with 6- to 9-foot crosscut saws. The swamp forest was filled with the sounds of grunting men, slashing saws, and the cracking, crashing, and tremendous thuds of falling giants. The toppled trees were trimmed and then dragged to the trams, a dangerous process. From a stationary locomotive that held a large rotating drum known as a power skidder, horses pulled a cable or wire rope to the fallen timber. Men attached the loose end to a log, and the skidder was cranked up. Everything in the path of the huge moving log was destroyed— young trees and plants—as it plowed through the swamp's soft bottom. The tension on the cable was tremendous. A break could mean maiming or death for men or horses in the way of the flying cable. Logging accidents were frequent. The devastation to the rich bottomland forest was unimaginable. Once dragged parallel to the tracks, the cypress logs were loaded onto rail cars with cranes and taken to the sawmill.

A logger's day often began with a wake-up call or whistle at 4:30 a.m. Breakfast usually consisted of fried fat pork, biscuits, syrup, and coffee. Around 6:00 a.m., a train carried the loggers to the work area, and then back to camp after ten or twelve hours of hard work. A pay of twenty-five cents an hour for most workers was given nightly by the Burton-Swartz Cypress Company of Perry. Entertainment, for those who still had energy, often took the form of drinking and gambling.

In the logging town of Carbur, 17 miles south of Perry, a 1928 account states that a vacant space separated the white and black sections of town. "Two clubhouses are provided for the Negroes," wrote the author. "One for the pious folks whose chief amusement is lodge and revival meetings, and another at the other side of the quarters for those Negroes who wish to dance, shoot craps, and carry on in a lighter vein than that offered by the brethren of the cloth."

When the heyday of logging virgin timber ended in Taylor County, marked by the liquidation of the Burton-Swartz Cypress Company of Florida in 1942, the local economy was devastated. Many loggers relocated to the dwindling stands of virgin cypress in south Florida, where cutting had begun in earnest. Perry continued to play a role, however, when entrepreneurs devised a way to ship cypress logs from the Everglades to Perry for sawing.

After Buckeye Cellulose Corporation opened its plant on the Fenholloway in 1954, a new era of pulpwood production began. Pine trees were soon planted and harvested like row crops in highly mechanized operations. And cypress trees, once cut by hand at great risk and prized for making durable lumber and shingles, are now often timbered at a young age and ground into garden mulch. Consumers have the mistaken impression that young cypress wood has the same rot- and termite-resistant qualities as old-growth cypress lumber, but it may take centuries for a cypress to develop those qualities. It is now believed that cypress trees in Florida are being cut at a rate faster than they can naturally grow or regrow. Conservationists are urging consumers to purchase pine bark or melaleuca mulch (made from an invasive exotic species) to reduce the pressure to clear-cut Florida's wetlands for a second time.

Times have changed for the lumber industry and forested lands of Taylor County, but Tide Swamp is regaining a semblance of its former majesty. When I wander its cypress groves in April, the spring beauty doesn't allow me to dwell on the past. Stumps, ditches, and ruts from cutting and skidders are cloaked in flowers, ferns, and butterflies—living testaments to the cycle of renewal. And the parklike stands of cypress and gum, while not massive, whisper in salty breezes and are filled with the music of singing birds.

Since Tide Swamp—as part of the Big Bend Wildlife Management Area—is in the public domain, I have little worry that its second-growth forest will be logged, or that people will rip out the sabal palms to sell to large developments seeking a classic "Florida look." I feel confident that I can grow old with an unmarred Tide Swamp, and that cypress trees will flourish long after I'm gone.

15

THE CEDAR KEYS

An eclectic mix of people, speaking English, French, German, and Japanese, mingled along Cedar Key's wide public pier. Some snapped photos, others tried their hand at fishing; all seemed to appreciate the magnificent view of wild tree-covered islands that made up the Cedar Keys National Wildlife Refuge.

John Muir once described Cedar Key as "surrounded by scores of other keys, many of them looking like a clump of palms, arranged like a tasteful bouquet, and placed in the sea to be kept fresh." The observation still rings true.

The closest island from my south-facing vantage point was Atsena Otie, only a half mile away. Once a bustling extension of Cedar Key, it is now uninhabited. The alluring island, with its sandy beach and mass of green trees and plants, looked similar to the many islands Liz and I had encountered at the end of our paddling trip. Some day we expect the Big Bend Paddling Trail to be lengthened to Cedar Key or beyond. It would be a fitting endpoint, not only because of Cedar Key's present-day role as tourist mecca for those seeking peace, beauty, seafood, and fishing, or because of the change in geography from a shallow, marsh-lined coast to island clusters and deeper water, but because of its former role as a cutting-edge frontier town.

In the 1880s, Cedar Key emerged as a boomtown, a bustling port city. A great pageantry of sailing vessels and steamships filled the harbor, many bearing the multicolored flags of other countries. Steam locomotives carrying supplies and passengers chugged across bridges to the four keys that

A lone fisherwoman tries her luck along the historic wharf of Cedar Key. Once a bustling port city labeled "the toughest town in the South," Cedar Key now appeals to tourists for most of its income.

make up the town. Throngs of sailors and visitors frequented seaside saloons, bordellos, gambling establishments, and dance halls. And like frontier towns of the West, most men carried one to two pistols and a bowie knife for offense or defense. Skirmishes were frequent, prompting one travel writer to label Cedar Key "the toughest town in the South." It was Dodge City, Gulf Coast style, though promoters preferred to bill it as "the Venice of Florida."

I often wonder if my great-grandfather Nagy visited Cedar Key during its heyday. He was a sailor in the Austro-Hungarian navy, back in the late 1800s. He eventually jumped ship in Apalachicola, another bustling port at the time. With help from local citizens, he joined in the lucrative alligator hunting trade along the Apalachicola River and Bay. He eventually made his way to Chicago, whereupon he sent for his family. Thinking of great-grandfather gives me a sense of full circle when I return to the Big Bend coast. The Big Bend coast was an embarking point for many like him who sought the proverbial American Dream.

What helped to fuel Cedar Key's economic boom were coastal cedars. Logging crews scoured the coast and tidal swamps in search of commercial-size trees. Cedar logs were rafted together and floated to sawmills in Cedar

Key, to be cut into slats and shipped to northern pencil factories. Cypress and pine logs were also processed and sold. During peak production in the 1880s, Cedar Key exported more than a million cubic board feet of finished lumber annually.

Cedar Key also marketed sea turtles, oysters, mullet, and sponges. Six hundred- to eight-hundred-pound green turtles were commonly taken, with one believed to have topped a thousand pounds. Like the old-growth trees, all were finite resources; all were exploited to the point of diminishing returns. Town and business leaders realized, a bit late, that bounties of the land and sea had their limits. It is a familiar story throughout the Big Bend and Florida, and throughout the world, one that inexplicably continues today.

Muir's long ago writings seem especially relevant when considering the hell-bent way we are using up the world's oil, or pushing a legion of creatures toward the abyss of extinction: "it never seems to occur to these far-seeing teachers that Nature's object in making animals and plants might possibly be first of all the happiness of each one of them, not the creation of all for the happiness of one. Why should man value himself as more than a small part of the one great unit of creation? And what creature of all that the Lord has taken the pains to make is not essential to the completeness of that unit—the cosmos?"

Two other major factors contributed to Cedar Key's decline in the late 1800s. The town lost out to Tampa as a major port, partly because the harbor's channel was considered too narrow and shallow for newer, steel-hulled ships, and wharf space was limited. Moreover, tourists began bypassing the city, enticed by railroads and accommodations created by the Walt Disneys of their day: Henry Flagler of the east coast and Henry Plant of the west. A killer hurricane added an exclamation point to the rapid demise. In the twentieth century, the town evolved into a quaint fishing village.

More recently, in response to the gill net ban and other changes, resourceful residents have developed a thriving clam industry. Tourism has also flourished. Brothels and saloons that once dominated the waterfront have given way to seafood restaurants and gift shops. The past is not all forgotten, however. Ghost stories abound, from tales of a headless horseman pirate to more subtle sightings. Their telling is partly to thrill tourists, I suspect, but not all.

One tale is described by Cecille Hulse Matschat in *Suwannee River:*

Strange Green Land, part of the renowned Rivers of America series published in 1938. In this tale, Matschat describes herself in the third-person as "The Plant Woman." She learned the tale at a Cedar Key barbecue of roast hog, duck, chicken, and fish chowder held in her honor.

Presently the Plant Woman asked a question about storms on the Gulf. Captain Portygee admitted that bad blows, and hurricanes too, struck the waters, which today looked as blue and peaceful as the heavens; but, he said, few fishermen were lost even in the worst gales because of the *Lura Lou.*

The Plant Woman leaned forward. "What is the *Lura Lou*?" she asked eagerly.

"*Lura Lou* is a phantom ship," Pompano explained. "She comes alus in time of very bad storm when there is great danger to fishermen out there. The *Lura Lou* calms the water round the fishing boats and brings them safe to port."

"Do you mean that, even in a hurricane, this ghost ship appears and there is calm water around the boats?"

"Dat's right." Captain Portygee nodded his head sagely. "No matter how hard wind blow, soon as Luck an' *Lura Lou* come, what she calm down an' boats ride home."

On one of our earlier coastal kayaking excursions, Liz had told me a spooky story of the time she paddled the short distance to Atsena Otie Key, once the site of a thriving town and now part of the wildlife refuge. "I was up real early and nobody was out yet," she began. "I paddled over to Atsena Otie. You can easily tell if anybody is there because there's really only one beach; there's a long wharf where the ferry comes over a couple of times a day. It's a small place. I docked my boat and started walking around. I was kind of musing on the layers of history of the place, all the different eras of people who have been there—the Indians, Civil War, Spanish, just layer after layer of people have been there. I walked over to the old cemetery, which is kind of a movie-set; it's really picturesque—all these leaning headstones and old rusted grillwork and little fences, and Spanish moss along the edge of the lagoon. It's really cool.

"I walked around a little bit and started walking back to where I left my kayak, coming up through the old town site before the hurricane blew it away and they moved it to the mainland, and I stopped to read this interpretive sign about the history. I'm standing there, and I could hear somebody whistling. It was a nice, sort of mindless whistle, like you're mending a net or doing some gardening, just doing some sort of chore on a beautiful sunny day and you're whistling, and I thought, cool. Somebody's here. I wanted to find out who it was. I walked down to the beach and there's my boat, and there's not another damn person in sight. There's nobody anywhere doing any whistling. I kind of got the feeling of 'oh, damn, I'm not alone.' It wasn't really scary, not the headless horseman pirate, but I kind of felt uneasy and got in my boat and split."

For some reason, Liz's tale tickled my boyhood sense of curiosity and adventure. I had to visit Atsena Otie and see, feel, or hear for myself. On a clear May morning, I launched my one-person canoe from the sandy shores of the city park. I sometimes prefer the openness of a canoe to a kayak for short trips, although I use a kayak paddle to propel the 10-foot craft. My first thought upon entering Cedar Key's harbor was that tourism is great until you have to paddle against a headwind in a small, self-propelled craft while rising and falling in the wake of numerous powerboats. From a harbor that had once been filled with ships that had a distinct purpose—to load or unload goods and supplies—the waters of Cedar Key are now filled with pleasure craft of all types, including tour boats with names such as *Island Hopper.*

I landed on Atsena Otie and walked a sandy beach covered with oyster shells from eroding Indian middens and brick pieces from later settlers. Occasionally, I spotted smooth black sherds of hand-molded pottery. I passed a group of children who shrieked excitedly as they caught hermit crabs in the water, surely an activity that generations of children have enjoyed on Atsena Otie.

On a marked trail, I entered the island's interior and passed the brick ruins of Eberhard Faber's cedar mill, where workers were paid thirty-five cents a day to cut and pack cedar slats. The factory site was covered with junglelike growth—vines, sabal palms, live oaks, and, appropriately, cedar trees. It always amazes me how nature can reclaim a place.

Moving down the picturesque trail, the twisted arms of live oaks and umbrellalike sabal palms offered a cool canopy. I admired flaming red blooms of coral bean, and the paddle-shaped segments of prickly pear cactus. I reached the cemetery on the east end of the island; the graves were situated on a live oak–covered hill facing the sunrise. They have a beautiful

The cemetery on the island of Atsena Otie, near Cedar Key, is all that remains of a once-thriving village. By the dates on the tombstones, it was apparent that many early residents had died in clusters, most likely of malaria, cholera, or yellow fever.

view of eternity, I thought, with the omnipresent sounds of red-winged blackbirds along the marsh fringe and the whistles of osprey. To the north I could see a clear view of the new condominiums on Cedar Key's southeastern boundary, named after a sawmill that once occupied the spot—Old Fenimore Mill. The shiny development seemed strangely out of place on an island that prides itself on historic structures and architecture. At least Atsena Otie would be spared a similar fate, I thought. In the mid-1980s, Depot Key Venture Corporation planned a modern subdivision on the island. Conservationists hotly contested the plan. The island was purchased by the state in 1997 under Florida's Preservation 2000 program, with management transferred to the United States Fish and Wildlife Service.

Perhaps the only sad thing for those buried on the island is that their graves are now a curiosity, their tombstones to be studied and gazed upon by countless visitors, with folks such as myself wondering how they died. For example, did Georgia Lewis perish from difficulties in labor? She died three days after her son, Wm Jones Lewis, was born. The infant son died three months later and was buried alongside his mother. Since it was Mother's Day, I thought of the total sacrifice mothers sometimes make for their children.

Mary Fagan is also buried on Atsena Otie. In her day, there was a little ditty people sang about her: "Little Mary Fagan went to town one day. She went to the pencil factory to collect her little pay." I can picture children jumping rope to the tune.

By the dates on the tombstones, it was apparent that many had died in clusters, probably of malaria, cholera, or yellow fever. John Muir concluded that "no portion of this coast, nor of the flat border which sweeps from Maryland to Texas, is quite free from malaria. All the inhabitants of this region, whether black or white, are liable to be prostrated by the ever-present fever and ague, to say nothing of the plagues of cholera and yellow fever that come and go suddenly like storms, prostrating the population and cutting gaps in it like hurricanes in woods."

John Muir could easily have been one of the victims. To his fortune, he met a kind Cedar Key family immediately upon conclusion of his 1,000-mile walk to the Gulf. "Mr. Hodgson's family welcomed me with that open, unconstrained cordiality which is characteristic of the better class of Southern people," he wrote. He felt queasy the next day, and malarial fever struck him two days later. "I rose, staggered, and fell, I know not how many times, in delirious bewilderment, gasping and throbbing with only moments of consciousness. Thus passed the hours till after midnight, when I reached the mill lodging-house." With quinine and calomel, the Hodgson family nursed Muir back to health over the course of three months.

During his recovery, Muir became enchanted with coastal live oaks and shorebirds: "During my long sojourn here as a convalescent I used to lie on my back for whole days beneath the ample arms of these great trees, listening to the winds and the birds. There is an extensive shallow on the coast, close by, which the receding tide exposes daily. This is the feeding-ground of thousands of waders of all sizes, plumage, and language . . . herons white as wave-tops, or blue as the sky, winnowing the warm air on wide quiet wing;

pelicans coming with baskets to fill, and the multitude of smaller sailors of the air, swift as swallows, gracefully taking their places at Nature's family table for their daily bread. Happy birds!"

Had Muir not recovered, Yosemite National Park may never have been established, and many of America's other cherished wild areas may have fallen under the axe and bulldozer. Muir always felt indebted to the Hodgsons for saving his life, and in 1898, thirty-one years after his first visit, he returned to Florida to pay tribute. Mr. Hodgson and his son had passed away by then, but he found Mrs. Hodgson living in Archer, Florida. In a letter to his wife, Muir wrote: "I asked her if she knew me. She answered no, and asked my name. I said Muir. 'John Muir?' she almost screamed. 'My California John Muir?' I said, 'Why yes, I promised to come back and visit you in about twenty-five years, and though a little late I've come.'"

As I wandered the Atsena Otie cemetery, lizards and skinks scurried through the duff of oak leaves, their little scampering feet collectively sounding like the tiny rattle of a pygmy rattlesnake. Since the hike at Econfina River State Park on the first day of our paddling trip, I was always on the lookout for the small venomous reptiles.

I didn't see or hear any spirits—only the whistles of an osprey—but I did sense a presence; it gave me a prickly feeling. It was time to move on, I determined. Perhaps it was because the lifestyles of those who lived on the island had been far different from my own, and the people were not family.

I left the tilted tombstones feeling a need for grave medicine, made from crushed mint leaves, grape vine tendrils, and other plants. At the Muskogee Creek grounds, we wash ourselves with grave medicine if we have been to funerals or cemeteries. The medicine is intended to cleanse oneself of unwanted influences before the main ceremony begins. I vowed to use grave medicine at the next gathering.

As I followed the trail back across the island, I wondered about the real ghosts of Atsena Otie. Perhaps they are the coastal cedar trees, a species never replanted but left to recover from wild seed. The Muskogee people consider cedar a sacred tree. Long ago, the story goes, an exhausted Creator slept under a cedar tree after creating much of the world. During his slumber, the breath of Creator became infused with the cedar wood. To burn the fragrant cedar leaves or wood is to release Creator's breath.

It is interesting to think how the cedar tree was and still is used to create another form of magic—a writing instrument. At the Cedar Key Historical

Society Museum, an entire display explains the evolution of the pencil, and how people such as philosopher and naturalist Henry David Thoreau conceived an advanced pencil design and helped to run a New England factory that manufactured them.

Appropriately, the name Atsena Otie means "Cedar Island" in the Muskogee Creek tongue, although "Atsena" is misspelled and mispronounced. "Cedar" in Muskogee is "Vcenv," pronounced ah-jen-ah. The Spanish called the island Las Yslas Sabinas, also meaning Cedar Island, during their 250-year rule. In 1839, the United States Army established a supply depot and hospital for use during the Second Seminole War; unimaginatively, they called it Depot Key. Interestingly, at the war's conclusion in 1842, a major hurricane damaged most of the buildings. The army retreated. Only a handful of people lived on the island until 1860, when Faber's cedar mill was built. The mill's presence boosted the island's population from fewer than 50 to 297, according to the 1860 census.

The Union army occupied Atsena Otie during the Civil War, using it as a base to stop blockade-runners and to execute raids on Confederate saltworks. After the war, the island's cedar mill prospered until cedar stands up and down the coast were nearly exhausted by lumbering in the early 1890s. Once again, a major hurricane marked the end of an era. The 1896 storm devastated Faber's cedar mill and every other mill in the area.

The *Tampa Tribune Weekly* described the killer storm:

> At seven o'clock an immense tidal wave came in from the south carrying destruction with it. Boats, wharves, and small houses were hurled upon the shore. . . .
>
> The tidal wave caused the principal loss of life, many houses being swept from their foundations and the inmates drowned.

More than a hundred people lost their lives and hundreds more were homeless. With the railroad incapacitated, the mills destroyed, and the town in ruins, an estimated 2,500 people were out of work in the Suwannee valley. Considering the already declining economy, it must have seemed like a deathblow. People left Cedar Key in droves. Those who remained largely turned to the sea for their living, harvesting fish, oysters, and sponges. Atsena Otie, however, was soon abandoned. The surviving houses were moved by barge across the harbor to the higher hills of Cedar Key in 1904.

After the hurricane, Cedar Key's only stab at new industry was the opening of a brush factory in 1910. Workers turned out high-quality brushes and brooms made from palm fiber; production continued even through the Great Depression. But competition from inexpensive plastic brushes, coupled with—you guessed it—a deadly hurricane, this one in 1950, severely damaged the factory. It permanently folded two years later.

I returned to my canoe. The wind had calmed and, inexplicably, fewer boats plied the waters. My eyes followed the arrowlike flocks of white ibis as they flew toward nearby Seahorse Key. The island, once used as an army prison to house Seminole captives, is now one of the largest colonial bird rookeries along the Gulf coast. The nesting egrets, herons, and pelicans enjoy a panoramic view since the island's central ridge of 52 feet above sea level is the highest elevation on Florida's west coast.

The slicing fin of a bottlenose dolphin seemed to guide me across the harbor to a safe landing. I strolled Dock Street. After a quiet morning on Atsena Otie, Cedar Key's bustling waterfront, with its multilevel restaurants and gift shops, seemed a bit garish and tacky. The strip reminded me of Aspen and countless other towns in scenic locations that seek to lure visitors away from their money. But what helps to make the waterfront special, and all of Cedar Key for that matter, is that it continues to stand apart from Anywhere USA. There are no fast food restaurants, no giant box store chains, no Wal-Marts. Most of the businesses are unique and locally owned, and if I was in a more social, spendthrift mood, I would have been content to stay and part with some money. Instead, I retreated to the hilly downtown only blocks away with its slower pace, regal homes and businesses, and old-growth trees.

Utilizing a handy walking tour brochure, I wandered the streets. The oldest home I passed was built around 1860, one described as "a modified steamboat design" because the second-story resembled a wheelhouse reached by a winding stairway. I wondered if John Muir had spent time there.

I drove a twisting road to the northwestern end of Cedar Key—none of the roads connecting this cluster of islands run straight for long—and visited the approximate location of Hodgson's sawmill and home, where Muir had convalesced. Modern homes stand there today, and no trace of the mill could be seen, but the tidal coves appeared as wild as they did in Muir's day. Ibis poked along shorelines and red-winged blackbirds sang from shrubs. Lush, tree-covered keys were visible in every direction, and so were flocks of birds. A salty breeze kicked up, stirring the marsh grass; I drew in a long refreshing breath. All was blue and green and beautiful. I gave my thanks to those who had gone before—and to life!—and quietly left the ancient shoreline of the Big Bend coast, promising, as always, to return.

BIBLIOGRAPHY

Adams, Chuck, Steve Jacob, and Suzanna Smith. "What Happened after the Net Ban." Gainesville: University of Florida, Institute of Food and Agricultural Sciences, 1999.

Bartram, William. *Travels through North and South Carolina, Georgia, East and West Florida.* Philadelphia: James and Johnson, 1776.

Bohart Museum of Entomology. "No-see-ums." Davis: University of California. http://bohart.ucdavis.edu/content/insects/NoSeeUms.pdf.

Brown, Robin C. *Florida's First People.* Sarasota: Pineapple Press, 1994.

Buckeye Technologies. "Buckeye Announces Seagrass Study." Press release. July 7, 1998.

———. "Buckeye Effluent Tests Non-Detect for Dioxin." Press release. November 13, 2000.

———. "Environment." http://www.bkitech.com/environment/environment.htm.

Carr, Archie. *A Naturalist in Florida.* New Haven and London: Yale University Press, 1994.

———. *The Sea Turtle: So Excellent a Fishe.* Garden City, N.Y.: Natural History Press, 1967.

Cash, W. T. "Taylor County History and Civil War Deserters." *Florida Historical Quarterly* 26 (July 1947–April 1948): 28–49.

Cedar Key Historical Society. "Old Cedar Key Walking Tour." Booklet. Rev. ed. Booklet. Cedar Key, 1999.

Chanton, Jeffrey. "Global Warming and Florida." *Florida Wildlife* (September–October 2002).

Connell, Vivian. "Mysterious Sidewalk Marks Bonita Beach." *Perry (Fla.) Taco Times,* July 10, 1985.

Cox, David. "Researchers: Slowing Boats Key to Manatees' Survival." Press Release. Tallahassee: Florida State University, March 2004.

De Vaca, Alvar Nuñez Cabeza. *Adventures in the Unknown Interior of America.* 1542. Albuquerque: University of New Mexico Press, 1983.

Dixie County Historical Society. *Cemeteries of Dixie County.* Old Town, 1996.

Dodd, Dorothy. *Florida in the War, 1861–1865.* Tallahassee: Peninsular Publishing, 1959.

Duryea, Mary L., and L. Annie Hermansen. "Cypress: Florida's Majestic and Beneficial Wetlands Tree." Circular 1186. Gainesville: University of Florida Cooperative Extension Service, n.d.

Elston, Suzanne. "Proctor and Gamble's Toxic Tea." Canada: WEED Foundation online newsletter. http://webhome.idirect.com/~born2luv/toxictea.html.

Eppes, Susan Bradford. *Through Some Eventful Years*. Macon, Ga.: J. W. Burke Company, 1926.

Faulkner, Gwen. "A Study of a Taylor County Feud." Paper submitted in English 473, Florida State University, December 9, 1969. Available at Taylor County Historical Society.

Fishburne, Charles Carroll, Jr. 1997. *The Cedar Keys in the Nineteenth Century*. Cedar Key: Cedar Keys Historical Society, 1997.

Florida Department of Environmental Protection, "Nontropical Reef Types and Associated Communities." http://www.dep.state.fl.us/coastal/habitats/seagrass/awareness_day/info3.htm.

Florida Marine Research Institute. "Florida's Seagrass Meadows." Brochure. St. Petersburg, March 2002.

———. "Horseshoe Crabs: Living Fossils." Sea Stats publication. St. Petersburg, November 2003.

———. "Loggerhead Nesting in Florida." http://www.floridamarine.org/features/view_article.asp?id=2411.

———. "Manatees: Florida's Gentle Giants." Sea Stats publication. St. Petersburg, May 1997.

———. "Manatee Mortality Data, 1974–2003." http://www.floridamarine.org/features/category_sub.asp?id=2241.

———. "Sea Turtles: Nomads of the Deep." Sea Stats publication. St. Petersburg, September 2002.

———. "They've Hatched! Rare Kemp's Ridleys Found on Clearwater Beach." http://www.floridamarine.org/features/view_related_articles.asp?Page=2&related=8259.

Florida Sea Kayaking Association. "Shark Attacks Kayak off Cumberland Island." http://www.fska.org/tooth.htm.

Frantzis, George. *Strangers at Ithaca: The Story of the Spongers of Tarpon Springs*. St. Petersburg: Great Outdoors Press, 1962.

Hampton Springs Club and Hotel. Early brochure. Taylor County Historical Society, n.d.

Harrington, Drew. "Burton-Swartz Cypress Company of Florida." *Florida Historical Quarterly* 62, no. 4 (April 1985): 423–33.

Hauserman, Julie. "Dioxin at Mill Too High." *St. Petersburg Times*, February 9, 2001.

Hendry, Norman C. *The Old Fenholloway*. Perry, Fla.: Bullock Music Print, 1951.

Hoese, H. Dickson. "Jumping Mullet—The Internal Diving Bell Hypothesis." *Environmental Biology of Fishes* 13, no. 4 (1985): 309–14.

Hunt, Cynthia M. "The Dilemma of the Fenholloway River." Paper submitted in Environmental Health master's course, Florida A&M University, 2004.

Jackson, Andrew. Letters to Richard K. Call. Call Family Papers. Tallahassee: Florida Archives. http://www.floridamemory.com/Collections/CallBrevardPapers/Call-11.cfm.

Jenkins, Robert L., Elizabeth M. Wilson, Robert A. Angus, Mike W. Howell, Marion

Kirk. "Androstenedione and Progesterone in the Sediment of a River Receiving Paper Mill Effluent." *Toxicological Sciences* 73 (2003): 53–59.

Jones, Maxine D., Larry E. Rivers, David R. Colburn, Tom R. Dye, William W. Rogers. "The Rosewood Report History." Submitted to Florida Board of Regents, December 22, 1993.

Jones, Robert P. "Florida's Net Ban—A Study of the Causes and Effects." Southeastern Fisheries Association, 1995. http://www.southeasternfish.org/Documents/commfish.html.

Karakitsios, Evelyn. "Sponging in Taylor County." Perry, Fla.: Taylor County Historical Society, n.d.

Kennedy, Stetson. "A Florida Treasure Hunt." Washington, D.C.: American Folklife Center, Library of Congress, n.d. http://memory.loc.gov/ammem/flwpahtml/ffpres01.html.

———. *Palmetto Country.* Tallahassee: Florida A&M University Press, 1942.

Knox, Jerry G. "The Coontie Creeper." *Florida Wildlife* (May–June 2003): 28.

Lanier, Sidney. 1875. *Florida: Its Scenery, Climate, and History.* Gainesville: University of Florida Press, 1973.

Lawrence, Eleanor. "Fiddler Crabs See Predators above the Horizon." Science Update. *Nature,* 1998. www.nature.com/nsu/.

Loughridge, R. M., and David M. Hodge. *English and Muskogee Dictionary.* Philadelphia: Westminster Press, 1914.

Lovel, Leo. *Spring Creek Chronicles.* Tallahassee: privately published, 2000. (To order online: www.florida-secrets.com/florida_bed-and-breakfast/Florida_Books/Real/Stories/Fish.htm)

Mahmoudi, Dr. Behzad. "Striped Mullet: Florida's Jumping Fish." St. Petersburg: Florida Marine Research Institute, 2003.

Mahon, John K. *History of the Second Seminole War, 1835–1842.* Gainesville: University Press of Florida, 1967.

Markham, Adam. *Trouble in Paradise: The Impacts of Climate Change on Biodiversity and Ecosystems in Florida.* Washington D.C.: World Wildlife Fund, July 2001.

Matschat, Cecile Hulse. *Suwannee River: Strange Green Land.* New York: Rinehart, 1938.

Muir, John. *A Thousand-Mile Walk to the Gulf.* Boston and New York: Houghton Mifflin, 1916.

Munro, David. "The Biogeography of the Monarch Butterfly." San Francisco: San Francisco State University, Department of Geography, Fall 1999. http://bss.sfsu.edu/geog/bholzman/courses/fall99projects/Monarch/monarch.htm.

National Archives. War Correspondence Files. Fort Stansbury discharge requests compiled by E. Raye Rainer, Taylor County Historical Society. Washington, D.C.

Natural Resources Defense Council. *Feeling the Heat in Florida.* New York, October 2001.

Nature Conservancy. "Using Doppler Radar to Save Songbirds." http://nature.org/magazine/summer2002/doppler/.

Nellis, David W. *Poisonous Plants and Animals of Florida and the Caribbean.* Sarasota: Pineapple Press, 1997.

"No-See-Ums: More Than Just an Irritation." *Undercurrent Magazine,* January 2000. http://www.undercurrent.org/UCnow/articles/NoCM200001.shtml.

"Old Taylor Logging Camps . . . The Way They Were." *Perry (Fla.) Taco Times,* circa 1980.

Paisley, Clifton. *The Red Hills of Florida, 1528–1865.* Tuscaloosa: University of Alabama Press, 1989.

Pasco County Extension Office. "Cypress Mulch?" http://mastergardeners.pasco gardening.com/page13.html.

Porter, Kenneth W. *The Black Seminoles: History of a Freedom-Seeking People.* Gainesville: University Press of Florida, 1996.

Powell, J. C. *The American Siberia.* Chicago: H. J. Smith, 1891.

Purdue University School of Veterinary Medicine. "Ohio Buckeye Horsechestnut." http://www.vet.purdue.edu/depts/addl/toxic/plant44.htm.

Raloff, Janet. "Macho Waters." *Science News* 159, no. 1 (January 6, 2001). www.mindfully.org/water/Hormone-River-Pollution.htm.

Rothchild, John. "The Day Drugs Came to Steinhatchee." *Harper's* (January 1983): 45–52.

Rudloe, Anne. "Horseshoe Crab." In *Coastal Marshes and Dunes: Guide to Outdoor Recreation and Conservation. Tallahassee Democrat,* 2002.

Rudloe, Jack. *The Living Dock.* Golden, Colo.: Fulcrum Press, 1988.

———. *Potluck.* Williamston, Mich.: Out Your Backdoor Press, 2003.

———. "Return of the Ridley." *Florida Wildlife* (September–October 2003): 26–27.

Sierra Club. John Muir exhibit. San Francisco. http://www.sierraclub.org/john_muir_exhibit/.

Staats, Eric. "Deep Trouble: Gone with the Grass." *Naples Daily News,* October 3, 2003.

Stewart, Charles W. "Official Records of the Union and Confederate Navies in the War of the Rebellion." Washington, D.C.: Government Printing Office, 1903.

Stolzenburg, William. "Swan Song of the Ivory-bill." *Nature Conservancy,* Fall 2002.

Swanton, John R. *The Indians of the Southeastern United States.* Washington and London: Smithsonian Institution Press, 1946.

Trenary, Charles. "Hampton Springs Hotel Remembered." *Taylor County News,* n.d.

Union of Concerned Scientists and the Ecological Society of America. *Confronting Climate Change in the Gulf Coast Region.* October 2001.

U.S. Department of Commerce. "March 1993 Winter Storm." Report. May 10, 1993.

U.S. Fish and Wildlife Service, Division of Endangered Species. "Gulf Sturgeon." http://daphne.fws.gov/sturgeon/sturgeon.html.

Vickers, Raymond B. *Panic in Paradise: Florida's Banking Crash of 1926.* Tuscaloosa and London: University of Alabama Press, 1994.

Warner, Daniel A. "The Horseshoe Crab in Florida." *Florida Wildlife* (July–August 2003).

Waters, Steve. "Net (ban) Success." *Ft. Lauderdale Sun-Sentinel,* July 2, 2000.

Weidensaul, Scott. "Across the Gulf on a Wing and a Prayer." *Nature Conservancy* (Spring 2004) http://nature.org/magazine/spring2004/features/art12063.html.

Whitney, Ellie, D. Bruce Means, and Anne Rudloe. *Priceless Florida: Natural Ecosystems and Native Species.* Sarasota: Pineapple Press, 2004.

Williams, Lindsey, and U. S. Cleveland. *Our Fascinating Past: Charlotte Harbor, The Early Years.* Punta Gorda, Fla.: Charlotte Harbor Area Historical Society, 1993.

Williams, Robert D. "Yellow Buckeye." USDA Forest Service. http://wildwnc.org/trees/Aesculus_octandra.html.

Williams, Ted. "Fiddler on the Marsh." *Audubon Earth Almanac,* National Audubon Society, 2001. http://magazine.audubon.org/earthalmanac/almanac0105.html#fiddler.

Wynne, Lewis N. "Pigs Will Wallow in the Streets: The Rise and Demise of Cedar Key as Florida's Port City." *Gulf Coast Historical Review* (Fall 1994): 44–59.

Ziewitz, Katherine, and June Wiaz. *Green Empire: The St. Joe Company and the Remaking of Florida's Panhandle.* Gainesville: University Press of Florida, 2004.

Interviews

Brashears, Julie. Personal meetings and communication. Tallahassee, 2003, 2004.

Chavous, Preston. Personal meeting. Munden Camp, Fla., 2004.

Cline, Evonne. Personal meeting. Old Town, Fla., 2004.

Curtis, Michelle. Telephone conversation. Perry, 2004.

Hauserman, Julie. Personal communication. Tallahassee, 2004.

Hayes, Bob. Personal communication. Tallahassee, 2004.

Hayes, Jamie. Personal meetings and communication. Tallahassee, 2003.

Magnum, Alice (Shug). Personal meeting and separate conversation recorded by Liz Sparks. Perry, 2003.

Mahmoudi, Dr. Behzad. Personal communication. St. Petersburg, Florida Marine Research Institute, 2004.

Morgan, Lucy. Personal communication. Tallahassee, 2004.

Penton, Dan. Personal meetings. Tallahassee, late 1980s–2004.

Rudloe, Jack. Personal meetings and communication. 2003, 2004.

Walsh, Mike. Personal meeting. SeaWorld Orlando, 2001.

Doug Alderson has authored numerous magazine articles and essays and is the winner of a first-place writing award from the Association for Conservation Information. A former associate editor of *Florida Wildlife* magazine, he currently works for the Florida Department of Environmental Protection as the field director for the Florida Circumnavigation Saltwater Paddling Trail, a planned sea kayaking trail around the entire state.

Related-interest titles from University Press of Florida

Al Burt's Florida: Snowbirds, Sand Castles, and Self-Rising Crackers
Al Burt

Beach and Coastal Camping in Florida
Johnny Molloy

From the Swamp to the Keys: A Paddle Through Florida History
Johnny Molloy

Gladesmen: Gator Hunters, Moonshiners, and Skiffers
Glen Simmons and Laura Ogden

Green Empire: The St. Joe Company and the Remaking of Florida's Panhandle
Kathryn Ziewitz and June Wiaz

Highway A1A: Florida At the Edge
Herbert L. Hiller

Kayaking the Keys: Fifty Great Paddling Adventures in Florida's Southernmost Archipelago
Kathleen Patton

Paddler's Guide to the Sunshine State
Sandy Huff

Seasons of Real Florida
Jeff Klinkenberg

Surrounded on Three Sides
John Keasler

Swamp Song: A Natural History of Florida's Swamps
Ron Larson

Voices of the Apalachicola
Faith Eidse

For more information on these and other books, visit our Web site at www.upf.com.